LOG CABIN PIONEERS

~Stories, Songs & Sayings~

by

Wayne Erbsen

Blue Ridge Heritage Archives, Ferrum College

*"The reason we have so few great men nowadays
is that there are so few log cabins for them to be born in."*
Chilson D. Aldrich, 1928

Order No. NGB- 955   ISBN: 1-883206-36-7
Library of Congress Control Number: 2001087783
©2001 by Native Ground Music, Inc.
Asheville, North Carolina

CONTENTS

CONTENTS

CONTENTS

CONTENTS

THE TRAIL TO MY OWN CABIN

It was the songs about log cabins that first captured my attention. As I was learning to play the banjo, the fiddle and the guitar, nearly forty years ago, I was drawn to the songs about log cabins. Perched high on a hill, a log cabin was something real and yet mysterious, something worth singing about. Of course, I eventually went on to learn a wide variety of American folk music. Still, songs about log cabins continued to hold a special fascination for me.

Perhaps my own interest in log cabins had more than a little to do with the fact that I grew up not in a humble cabin, but in a comfortable home in Southern California. Singing about cabins and the lifestyle they represented took me far from the city lights of California to the remote mountains of North Carolina and Virginia. As I began learning this music, I became more and more fascinated with the old-time lifestyles and folklore of people who grew up in pioneer settings.

Even as I was delving deeper into the music and lore of early America, I began studying American history in an academic setting. First, I earned a B.A. degree in American History at the University of California at Berkeley. I then went on to graduate study in history at the University of Wisconsin at Madison, where I earned a Masters degree. It wasn't until the first semester of graduate school that it

"He'd cross hell on a rotten log."

TRAIL TO MY OWN CABIN (CONT.)

dawned on me that my deep interest in American folk music was but a part of a deeper interest in history.

My hobby of folk music and my academic studies all came together when I admitted to one of my history professors that I played music. An avid folk music fan, he offered me a deal I couldn't refuse. Instead of writing a massive term paper on labor history like the rest of the class, the professor proposed that I get up in front of my classmates and sing old labor songs from the I.W.W., better known as the Industrial Workers of the World. Since my Mama didn't raise a dummy, I readily agreed. While the other students were struggling with writing a huge research paper, I got off easy by merely bringing my guitar to class and singing songs like "Solidarity Forever," "Union Maid," and a number of songs by the legendary I.W.W. songwriter, Joe Hill. The teacher was delighted, the class had a break from another boring lecture, and I had a light bulb go on in my mind. Forever after, my folk music and American history interests were merged.

University of North Carolina at Chapel Hill

"Our land's so poor, it wouldn't raise a fight."

TRAIL TO MY OWN CABIN (CONT.)

The music did more than focus my interests. It made me realize that I was living in the wrong place! I needed to live in the mountains of North Carolina or Virginia, where I could dig deep into the roots of Appalachian music and culture. So that's what I did. In 1972, I loaded up my vintage Volvo sedan and headed to the Southeast. I eventually wound up in Asheville, North Carolina, which became my permanent home. A year and a half ago, my wife Barbara and I even purchased a remote old log cabin, known as "The Old Crawford Place," to use as a getaway.

Log Cabin Pioneers is both a personal story as well as a collection of authentic stories, songs and sayings. It includes tall tales, jokes, remedies, superstitions, recipes and even insults. The scope of the book is wide. It begins with the early log cabin pioneers in the 1700's and ends in the late 1940's when the last pioneers died or joined the modern age. Geographically, the book will draw on songs, stories and folklore from every state that ever produced a log cabin.

University of North Carolina at Chapel Hill

To illustrate just how recently log cabin pioneers existed, I'll relate a story that happened to me just three days ago. While researching photos in the Appalachian Collection at Mars Hill College in Mars Hill, North Carolina, I delved into a rare collection that isn't even open yet to the general public. Buried deep inside the collection of

"Beauty draws more than oxen." (1876)

TRAIL TO MY OWN CABIN

old photos was a striking print of two pioneer women (below). Thinking the photo was a hundred years old or more, I showed it to the librarian, who then called over a gentleman who was doing research on the other side of the small reading room. "Take a look at what this gentleman found," pointing both to me and to the photo she held in her hand. The fellow got up and walked over. "Well I'll be darned!" he said. "I've never seen that photo before in all my family research. Those ladies are kin to me." He went on to tell me about the two sisters who

Mars Hill College

lived in that old pioneer cabin until the late 1940's when they were way up in age. Their cabin had no windows, no electricity, no plumbing. They lived by subsistence farming the same way the earliest pioneers had lived. Here was further proof of just how recently log cabin pioneers had existed.

Pioneer Insult
"He was so lazy he wouldn't holler 'sooey'
if the hogs were eating his toes."[15]

THE OLD CRAWFORD PLACE

Very few of the locals in the deep mountains of Big Pine, North Carolina even remembered the cabin. Those who did, called it "The Old Crawford Place." The cabin was set so far back in the steep mountains that the sun practically set on it before it even rose. Though we hadn't even seen it yet, this rustic log cabin would soon play a big part in our lives. It would also be part of the inspiration for this book.

Photo by Wayne Erbsen

The Old Crawford Place

In the spring of 1999, my wife Barbara and I began looking for a remote and rustic old cabin to use for a get-away. Everybody thought we were crazy and told us we were twenty or thirty years too late. We got used to hearing that all the old cabins had either rotted away, or had been purchased and updated. Then Barbara noticed a little ad in the paper and she knew right away that "this was it!" I had my doubts. How could there be a historic log cabin on 65 acres, only one hour from our home in Asheville, North Carolina for a price we could afford? It must be a dump. When we called about the ad, the realtor told us it didn't have electricity and we said, "Great!" When she said it didn't have plumbing, we said, "That's even better. When can we look at it?"

"A big wife and a big barn will never do a man any harm."

THE OLD CRAWFORD PLACE (CONT.)

Getting to the cabin was not easy. Heading north from Asheville on highway 19/23, we left the highway at Weaverville and crossed the French Broad River. We then navigated over roads so crooked that we almost met our-selves coming back! While we drove deeper into the moun-tains, the winding road followed Big Pine Creek. Driving over the twisty road, we saw sights which we thought no longer existed. Scattered along the road were log tobacco barns and outbuildings. We even saw people plowing with mules! And for each mile we drove, it seemed like we were going farther and farther back in time. It was almost as if, mile by mile, our modern van was becoming first a wagon pulled by a horse, then a mule, and then a team of oxen. Even the road signs on the side roads we passed made us feel as if we were going back in time: Crooked Ridge Lane, Puncheon Camp Road, Horse Knob Drive, and Hawk Ridge Road.

When we arrived at the property, we couldn't even see the cabin for all the underbrush. We hiked up a steep hill past an old log barn on a path that once must have been a road, though you couldn't tell it now. We had to climb over scores of downed trees, brambles, branches and even wade a creek which crossed our path. When the trail made a sharp dogleg to the left, our eyes widened as we looked up in awe at the cabin sitting peacefully up ahead in a small clearing. Bar-bara and I both knew that here, at last, was the cabin we had been looking for, The Old Crawford Place.

THE OLD CRAWFORD PLACE (CONT.)

As we hiked toward it, we could not believe our eyes. It looked to be a perfectly preserved, historic log cabin. The tin roof had done its job well, keeping the weather off the hand-hewn, yellow poplar logs. When we pushed the door open, we were surprised to see a room full of furniture and personal effects. Several chairs were carefully arranged in front of the fireplace, and there was an old pair of shoes over by the door. Going into the downstairs bedroom, we found a winter coat lying on the bed, as if someone had just laid it down. There was even a raincoat hanging on a peg next to the back door. The kitchen sink was filled with dishes, though part of the kitchen floor was rotted out. We soon figured out that a pipe had burst, and the water had run over part of the floor for the past twenty-three years.

Photo by Wayne Erbsen

The Old Crawford Place

Standing inside the cabin, Barbara and I looked at each other and we knew we had to have it. We didn't even have to ask each other; we just knew. That same day, we made an offer on the cabin, and, thank goodness, it was accepted. We were thrilled and couldn't wait to roll up our sleeves and start working on the place.

THE OLD CRAWFORD PLACE

We soon started to try to unravel some of the mysteries surrounding the cabin. Who had built it, and who had lived there last? Except for the cob webs and mouse tracks, why did it look like someone just stepped outside for a moment and never returned?

From Ray Worley, the seventy-seven year old grandson of the man who built it, we learned that the cabin was built between 1875-80 by Dave Worley, whose family had lived in Big Pine for as long as anyone could remember. Dave and his wife had three sons, Calvin, Crawford and Aison. Dave eventually built and moved into a frame house nearby and gave the cabin to his son Crawford, who moved in there with his wife Emma. Crawford and Emma had two children, Effie, who was born in the cabin in 1914, and Dewey, who came along in 1920. Crawford and his family lived in the cabin and farmed the mountain land until 1938, when they moved to Marion, North Carolina, some 100 miles southeast of Big Pine.

The cabin sat empty for thirty-six years until a young man from Florida bought it in 1974. He replaced the windows, rebuilt the porch and generally fixed up the place. The cold, lonely winters were finally too much for this bachelor, and in 1976 he moved on, leaving behind most of his belongings. Why he waited almost twenty-five years to sell it is still a mystery. Perhaps he thought that one day he'd return to live there, but years passed and he never did return. Finally, he decided to sell, and we were the lucky ones to get it.

I had always wanted to write a book about log cabins, and at last I had a front porch to write it on!

"Even a blind pig will sometimes find a acorn."

THE LOG CABIN
SYMBOL OF THE FRONTIER

E ven more than a flintlock rifle or a coonskin cap, the log cabin has stood as the very symbol of frontier America. Its sturdy wooden walls and carefully laid chimney reflect the values of hard work and rugged individualism. For those of us living at the beginning of the 21st century, just the thought of a log cabin takes us back to a simpler America, when all a man needed to succeed was honesty, courage, self-reliance and gumption.

The idea of using the log cabin as a symbol of the Great American Dream can be traced to the nasty Presidential campaign of 1840. During the hotly contested race between Whig candidate William Henry Harrison and Democrat Martin Van Buren, Henry Clay sarcastically referred to Harrison:

"Give him a barrel of hard cider, and settle a pension of $2,000 a year on him, and our word for it, he will sit the remainder of his days in his log cabin by the side of the "sea-coal fire" and study moral philosophy!"

This was all Harrison's campaign needed to give it a "cause." It shrewdly embraced the images of the log cabin and hard cider as purely American institutions. Harrison, they claimed, was one of the "common people," who sprang from the humble beginnings of a log cabin. In fact, this was an outrageous contortion of the truth. Harrison, the old war hero of Tippecanoe, was not born in a log cabin at all, but in a two and a half story red brick mansion overlooking the James River. Harrison's only connection to a log cabin was that in his later years he purchased 600 acres in Ohio which

SYMBOL OF THE FRONTIER

contained a four-room house that had been built around a one-room log cabin. By the time of the 1840 election, however, this house had been expanded to 16 rooms and the land holdings had increased to 3000 acres. Hardly a hardscrabble squatter's cabin![27]

Unfazed by his Southern aristocratic roots, Harrison's campaign touted his log cabin connection for all it was worth. Even the dignified dandies of the Whig party threw off the trappings of opulence and embraced the images of log cabins and hard cider. Even a statesman like Daniel Webster publicly apologized for *not* being born in a log cabin, but took comfort in the fact that his older brothers and sisters had been. He then added,

"...*that cabin I annually visit, and thither I carry my children, that they may learn to honor and to emulate the stern and simple virtues that there found their abode...*"[47]

With the Whigs widely ballyhooing the log cabin as proof of their candidate's humble American origins, the entire country was caught in the grip of "log cabin fever." Log cabin songs were even printed in each issue of Horace Greeley's newspaper, which he renamed "The Log Cabin."

There is no doubt that William Henry Harrison won the office of Presidency in 1840 in part because he cleverly seized the image of the log cabin to convince common people that he was one of them. But long after the delegates had gone home and their campaign rhetoric was forgotten, the log cabin remained a potent symbol of frontier America.

LOG CABIN FOR SALE

The political campaign of 1840 generated a swell of popular interest in all things related to log cabins. Realizing its commercial potential, advertisers affixed the log cabin image to every imaginable product. A line of patent medicines hit the market which included Log Cabin Rose Cream for catarrh, Log Cabin Liver Pills (a laxative), and best of all was "Warner's Log Cabin Sarsparilla" that was advertised as "An Old Fashioned Roots and Herbs Preparation" that promised to cure:

> ...all blood disorders, general debility, stomach, liver, bowels, skin diseases, eruptions, boils, pimples, blotches, cancerous and syphilitic affections, rheumatism, neuralgia, female weakness, dyspepsia. $1.00 for 120 doses. Always gives satisfaction.[27]

In 1887, a grocer named J.P. Towle blended cane syrup and maple sugar and packaged it in a log cabin tin. His intent was actually to pay tribute to his boyhood hero, Abe Lincoln, but the result was Log Cabin Syrup, a legend in the food marketing industry.[27]

It is ironic that the image of the log cabin was used so successfully both in commercial advertising and to elect Presidents. It became a potent American symbol which represented strength, honesty, hard work and simple American values. People who actually lived in log cabins, who were often at the bottom of the economic ladder, must have thought it very strange that their poor dilapidated hovel was becoming an American icon.

"Close the door. Are you from North Carolina?"

BORN IN LOG CABINS

Both the famous and the infamous were all born in log cabins: Andrew Jackson, James K. Polk, Abe Lincoln, Daniel Boone, Davy Crockett, Sam Houston, George Custer, James Buchanan, William McKinley, George Washington Carver, Booker T. Washington, Jesse James, John Wilkes Booth.

Alice Lloyd College

Sarsaparilla

William Jennings Bryant, himself a teetotaler, was not above campaigning for votes in a saloon. One time he met an old drunk, who asked Bryant his advice in giving up alcohol. Bryant suggested, "When you get all the liquor you want, why don't you order sarsaparilla?"

Replied the drunk, "When I get all the liquor I want, I can't say 'sarsaparilla.'"[4]

Pioneer Insult
"He'd steal cracklings out of his mammy's fat gourd."[10]

LOG CABIN ORIGINS (CONT.)

Soon after arriving on America's shores, the earliest English settlers built crude huts to shelter them until a more permanent house could be built. Using sailcloth, tree branches, bark and brush, these first structures gave but little protection against the elements. Even though they were surrounded by thick forests, the English settlers apparently gave no thought to building their houses out of logs. With no prior experience in log construction, they instead tried recreating the type of house common in England at that time. Using what was known as half-timber construction, heavy timbers were used for framing, while sticks and mud were used to fill in between the timbers. In America, this technique was modified with only clapboards to cover the framing.

North Carolina Archives & History

"There is not a cabin but has ten or twelve children in it."
Itinerant preacher Charles Woodmason, ca. 1770

LOG CABIN ORIGINS (CONT.)

In the mid-seventeenth century, America's first log houses were built by Swedish people who settled on the Delaware River in New Sweden. Even though log construction was easier and sturdier than the half-timber houses the English settlers were building, the English apparently had little contact with the Swedes and so were not influenced to build their houses out of logs.

The next wave of immigrants were the Germans and Scots-Irish, who both settled to the west of the English in Pennsylvania. At first, Germans attempted to build half timber houses similar to those built by the English. But faced with a lack of sawmills to mill their lumber and the plentiful supply of logs, the Germans fell back on their medieval building customs and built log homes.

Mars Hill College

The Scots-Irish were Protestants from the Scottish lowlands who settled in Northern Ireland in about 1600. The homes they built were constructed out of stone, with sod or thatched roofs. After suffering years of oppression, many emigrated to America in search of opportunity and religious freedom. After landing in New England, most migrated first to Pennsylvania and New Jersey and then on to Maryland, Virginia, the Carolinas, and Tennessee. Many of the first homes built by the Scots-Irish in America were built of logs. They apparently imitated the log house building techniques

LOG CABIN ORIGINS

learned from their Swedish and Finnish neighbors in Delaware and their German neighbors in Pennsylvania.[55]

Although many Germans remained in eastern Pennsylvania, by the 1730's the majority joined the Scots-Irish and headed south and west. Together, the Scots-Irish and the Germans settled in Virginia, North Carolina, and east Tennessee. These groups blended together and each borrowed heavily from the other, both culturally and socially. The Scots-Irish learned further log cabin building techniques from the Germans, and the Germans learned much of the rich music and dance traditions of the Scots-Irish.

In adopting the log construction techniques of the Germans, the Scots-Irish made several important changes of their own. Rather than building their houses in the shape of a rectangle, the Scots-Irish built their homes closer to a square. Instead of the interior chimneys favored by the Germans, the Scots-Irish preferred the English style of building the chimney on the outside of the house. It was this type of square house with the outside chimney that became the typical log cabin.

University of North Carolina at Chapel Hill

"Appetite furnishes the best sauce." Herman Melville (1846)

GETTING THERE

The earliest settlers faced the daunting task of traveling through an unknown wilderness before arriving at the place where they would build a log cabin and start a new life. They knew they would need to get to their destination before the coming of winter. After that, it would be difficult to build even a temporary log cabin. While wagons were heavily loaded with everything needed to survive, a perilous journey lay ahead. They would face an untamed wilderness fraught with multiple dangers and serious obstacles. There were few maps and fewer still that could be counted on.

Without clearly defined roads, settlers tended to follow creeks and the wagon ruts of those who had gone before. Many followed animal and Indian trails that had existed for centuries. Though these trails usually took the best route, they were often narrow, and were always rough and winding. In dry weather these trails were dusty and after a big rain they were muddy and often impassible.

Essential Pioneer Equipment

Froe, single-bitted axe, broad axe, adze, hatchet, drawknife, shovel, pick, saw, augers, wedges, plow, hoe, scythe, pitch fork, gun, bullet mold, powder, lead, traps, washtub, cooking pots, bucket, chamber pot, dishes, lamp, cooking utensils, clothing, bedding, household goods, seeds, farm animals, fiddle.

GETTING THERE (CONT.)

Making the journey all the more difficult was the fact that settlers nearly always overloaded their wagons. The added weight meant a more difficult pull for oxen or mules, that strained under heavy loads. Even with men and women and all but the smallest children walking beside the wagon, the load often proved too heavy, and precious belongings had to be discarded along the way. This included everything from anvils to augers, bedsteads, cookstoves, grindstones, barrels and ploughs. With a load made lighter by discarding items alongside the road, both men and woman still had to push the wagon out of a mud hole or bog and up steep hills. A good day's travel was about six miles, and often it was half of that. Traveling even short distances could be a perilous and dangerous journey for man and beast. There were mountains to cross and rivers to ford. Flies and biting insects were pesky and constant companions.

After a hard day of traveling, the weary settlers were ready to camp for the night by mid to late afternoon. One of the younger men had earlier gone ahead to scout out a good place to camp. Often traveling on horseback, he would ride far ahead in search of a level camping spot that had fresh water, wood for fires and grass for grazing. When the wagons finally arrived at their camping place, there was an instant flurry of activity. For the men, there were oxen or mules to be unharnessed and doctored, and wood that had

GETTING THERE

to be cut and and split. If there was enough daylight left, the men went hunting to provide fresh meat for the evening meal. A lucky hunter might return with a deer or even a bear; an unlucky one would have to settle for a jack rabbit, a groundhog or a squirrel or two.

Meanwhile, the women were busy unloading the wagon. Pots and pans, cooking utensils, bedding and grumpy children all had to be taken down from the wagon. There were clothes that had to be mended, washed and hung up to dry, and a fire would have to be kindled and supper started. The older children would gather twigs and branches for the fire and fill the water bucket. The young children usually ran free, happy to be out of the bumpy wagon.

Although wagons were slow and cumbersome, they were practically the only means of transportation available to 19th century families traveling in the wilderness. There is one intriguing story of a husband and wife with two small children who set out from eastern Missouri to the western part of the state. Without a horse or mule, they traveled on foot, carrying all their belongings and even their two children![16]

Pioneer Insult
"She was as ugly as a mud fence after a hard rain."

A NEW LIFE IN THE WILDERNESS

Though there were unthinkable hardships traveling through an untamed and largely uncharted wilderness, there was also a certain excitement in going to a new land with seemingly unlimited possibilities. Enticed by the promise of unspoiled natural beauty, abundant wild game and fertile land that could be had practically for the asking, settlers were itching to get there and begin building a new life in the wilderness.

When settlers arrived at their new destination, they were often hungry, sometimes sick, and always exhausted. Before they could clear the land and harvest a crop, they survived by hunting, trapping, fishing and gathering. In the summer, there might be wild berries to pick, and in the fall lucky scavengers might find black walnuts, persimmons, mulberries, chestnuts and hickory nuts.

Go Up the Mountain

A nurse was visiting a school where everybody was related to everyone else. She called the children together and said, "All of you look like a bunch of dried apples. Your stock is running out. When you grow up, and get it in your head to go sparking, don't go up the creek, and don't go down the creek. Go over the mountain."[49]

TRAPPING SUPPER

Some unfortunate pioneers arrived at their new home sites low on gun powder and lead and often without traps to provide wild game for their hungry families. To survive under such harsh conditions, they had to rely on ingenuity and sheer courage. To catch fish, many followed Indian traditions by weaving funnel-shaped baskets which allowed fish to swim in, but not out.

To trap wild game such as turkeys, boar, groundhogs, muskrats and even bear, many built log pens. From outside of these pens they would dig an underground tunnel that would lead into the pen. Lured by bait scattered at the entrance to the tunnel and inside the pen, curious and hungry animals would emerge from the tunnel and be trapped inside the pen. Even though they could conceivably escape from the same tunnel that brought them into the pen, most became hopelessly trapped. Bears, for example, would merely circle around inside the pen, restlessly looking for a way out. Combining the use of traps and pens with hunting and gathering, most pioneers did manage to survive, though few got fat!

"The sweetest sound I ever heard was the sound of a banjo,
or the cork coming out of a jug."
Robert Glenn, North Carolina

EARLY CRUDE STRUCTURES

Even before a permanent log cabin could be built, early pioneers fashioned a crude structure similar to a rough lean-to. Known as a "half-faced camp," it was made from trees, branches, brush and bark, and was open on one side. A quilt or blanket usually covered the opening to keep out the rain and wind.

A small temporary cabin with a dirt floor was then put up. In place of a chimney, there was often a rough hole in the roof for the smoke to go out, but it also served for the rain and critters to come in. This first cabin was usually built out of small logs, which were easier to cut, carry and lay up. With most back country areas being so sparsely settled, help was hard to find, so logs had to be small enough for a man, his wife, and maybe his sons to handle.

In their haste to get their cabin finished, early settlers often did not even bother to remove the bark from the logs. This proved to be a mistake. The bark provided a comfortable environment for insects to live and also held in moisture, which promoted rot. The corners of these cabins were roughly notched and the ends of the logs often protruded unevenly. Occasionally, a careless cabin builder would even allow the end of some logs to stick out past the roof line, and this further promoted rot and deterioration. Little wonder this type of cabin has all but vanished.

Pioneer Insult
"He was so lazy he wouldn't work at a pie counter."[9]

SELECTING A SITE

After the family had settled into their temporary round log cabin, it was time to start planning a more permanent log house. When picking out a spot to construct their cabin, many pioneers preferred to build near rivers and streams. Those who chose not to locate close to a stream or a river needed to build near a good spring. Some settlers were fooled into thinking their wet weather spring could be depended upon all year long. Many were shocked when their spring went dry, and their cabins had to be abandoned for lack of water. It was only the wise settler who knew how to tell if a spring had enough flow to provide water through dry spells.

Besides building cabins near a good source of water, many faced their cabin east to get the morning sun on the front porch. They looked for a sheltered nook at the foot of a hill which would shield them from the cold winds and snowdrifts of winter. The prime level land was saved for a garden.

"There's more ways to kill a dog than choke him on biscuits."

ONLY AN AXE

S ome early log cabins were built top to bottom using no more than an axe. With a single-bitted axe, an experienced woodsman could chop down, bark and hew the logs, make skids to position the logs in place, and even rive shakes or clapboards for the roof. Using a single-bitted axe, a settler could make hardwood gluts or wedges out of locust or hickory to split puncheons for the floor. Axe handles even served as a measuring stick in laying out and finishing the cabin. Most axe handles were 3' long, so it was common for a cabin to be 18' on one side and 21' on the other. Because so much depended upon a log cabin builder's axe, great care was taken to protect it from damage. In severely cold weather, some woodsmen slowly warmed their axe by the fire to keep it from breaking.

Great Smoky Mountains National Park

Tools of a Well-Equipped Cabin Builder
Felling axe, broad axe, adz, froe, wooden maul, crosscut saw, auger, draw knife, chisel, jack plane, hammer, shovel.

FELLING THE TREES

After selecting a site and laying up pillars of rock for a foundation, the next task was to select and fell enough trees to build the cabin. The best time to cut down the trees was in the winter, when the sap was down. Due to the difficulty of moving such massive logs, the trees that were closest to the site were given high priority. Trees that shaded the garden were also cut down, although sometimes these trees were simply girded, which killed them. The tool of choice for felling trees was a freshly-sharpened cross-cut saw. Of course, many trees were commonly felled with a simple axe.

The most ideal trees for log cabin building were yellow or tulip poplar, cedar or chestnut because each resisted rot and decay. Oak was avoided because it was too heavy. Poplar was a particular favorite because it grew to be large in diameter and was both straight and tall. Poplar was also easy to hew and the trunk was often 30' tall before there was a limb. Some cabins in Ohio and Indiana were built of black walnut.

"Hard work pays off in the future. Laziness pays off now."

HEWING

I f the log cabin builder even toyed with the idea of building his home out of round logs, his wife set him straight in a hurry. It was bad enough that he had dragged her out of a civilized life in the city, but if she was going to live in the wilderness, by God, she was going to have a real house with flat walls. A round log cabin might be good enough for a temporary shelter, but it simply would not do to raise children in such a hovel. No sir! To her, any round log structure was a barn, a pig pen, or a corn crib.

Hewing the logs was a tough task, but a man who knew how to swing a broad axe could often hew up to twelve logs a day. Most logs were hewed where they fell because they were easier to move after they had been hewed. Legends tell that pioneers often waited to hew their logs for the months that began with "M," March and May.[32]

Before he began hewing, the pioneer used an axe or a hatchet to mark a straight line that would serve as a guide. Modern log cabin builders commonly use a chalk line, or even a chain saw to mark the line, but of course, these tools would have been unknown to a pioneer builder. Standing very close to the log, the pioneer would have the flat side of the broadaxe toward the log. Most of the broadaxes had a handle that was curved away from the log, to save a man's knuckles. To lessen the wear and tear on his broadaxe, he often put wood down on the dirt next to the log to keep his tool out of the rocks. Some builders raised the logs up on blocks and used a short 2' long axe handle instead of the customary 3' handle. After he had hewed all his logs, the pioneer then numbered the logs with an axe or hatchet so that the logs on opposite sides would match.[32]

"A lazy traveler makes a long journey."
James Fenemore Cooper (1827)

NOTCHING THE LOGS

Although a number of notching styles were used, the one that was most common was the half-dovetail. This was considered the best because the slope of the notch allowed rain to drain away, which kept the ends of the logs from rotting. Other notches included the full dovetail, the V-notch, the half notch, the diamond notch, the double notch and the saddle notch.

How to Notch the Corners of a Log Cabin

1. With a broad axe, hew the opposite sides of a log about 12" from the end, until both sides are flat.

2. Slope the top surface of the hewed logs to a 30-45° angle.

3. Set a second hewed log on top of the sloped log at a 45° angle, so that the end is flush with the bottom of the first log.

Great Smoky Mountains National Park

4. Set a straight edge along the angle of the bottom log and draw that angle on the side of the top log. Do the same thing on the other side of the log.

5. Hew out the top log so that it makes a snug fit with the bottom log.

6. Now you're ready to repeat this process on the top and bottom of all the corners.

You can also make a pattern that will insure uniformity of the corner notches. To make a pattern, notch a corner log, as in steps 1 and 2 above. Then cut out a pattern that is the shape of the notch, and use it to make the other notches.

THE HOUSE RAISING (CONT.)

T hough the pioneer prided himself on his independence and self-reliance, he was not physically capable of raising or laying up the logs without serious help. For this he would need a gang of strong men capable of heavy lifting. After he had his foundation laid out, his logs hewed and numbered, he sent word throughout the backwoods that he was having a house raising.

On the appointed day, neighbors started arriving at daybreak. Some traveled by wagon and horseback while others came on foot. Entire families came to the house raising, with the men toting axes and saws and the women bringing food. While the children played, the women caught up on the latest news of the day. Sometimes the women found time to quilt. Their most important task, however, was preparing a hearty meal for all the people who had gathered for the house raising.

"It is unlucky to start building on a Friday."

THE HOUSE RAISING

The men's first job was dragging the logs into place with teams of oxen, mules or horses. Logs then had to be hand carried to get them into position to be laid up. The usual method of carrying these heavy logs was by means of hand spikes. These were stout poles which were often shaped with a drawknife on the ends to make it easier to pry up the logs. Once the men managed to raise the logs, the poles were shoved under the logs as the men arranged themselves at opposite ends of the poles. Given the signal, the men lifted the logs and carried them into position. When it was time to let the log down, the men on one side rested their end of the handspike on a log and then gingerly went around the other side to help raise the log high enough so it would slide down the pole to the ground. From this came the expression "the short end of the stick."[10]

The massive sill logs were then placed on the piers or foundation, making sure that the logs were laid in square. These sill logs were slightly bigger in diameter than the other logs to give added strength to the structure. Once the sill logs were laid, they would be mortised and floor joists would be laid in. The first two end logs were then notched flat on the bottom to fit the sills.

Pioneer Insult
*"What she lacks in beauty is more than
made up in ugliness."*[54]

LAYING UP

At least ten men working together were needed to lift logs into place. If fewer men were working, levers were cleverly used to lift the logs. When the walls had reached shoulder height, skids were brought in, which were cut out of stout poles or small trees. These skids would rest on the last log to be laid up, while the next log was pulled or pushed into place. Ropes or chains were then attached to the logs and pulled up by oxen or horses, while the men guided the logs into position. This process continued until all four walls were up.[1] To build a single-pen two-story cabin, it generally took a total of 9 logs per side, or 36 logs total.

Harper's Weekly, January 24, 1874

The amount of time it took to lay up the walls, of course, depended on the size of the cabin and the experience of the builders. One tale claimed that in two days, three men built a complete cabin. They felled and trimmed the trees, dragged the logs to the house site, notched them and erected a one room cabin complete with chimney and fireplace.[55] And all that without breaking a sweat!

"If you don't cuss, you'll never raise gourds."

FIDDLING UP A CABIN

Almost as important as the actual work of raising the logs, house raisings were a rare and festive community gathering. Men joked and told stories; women visited and gossiped; the young folks played, and the eligible young adults courted. Sometimes it seemed that the house raising was only an excuse for a much needed celebration. A fiddler was always welcomed as a necessary part of any cabin or barn raising. His task was to "fiddle up the cabin." He often played while the men worked, and sometimes he led the men in songs while he played the fiddle. Some people claimed "You couldn't put up a cabin or barn without the help of a fiddler." At the end of a long day of laying up the logs, music, celebration and feasting, a dance was always held. Many times, the only musician to play for a dance was a lone fiddler, who played such reels as "Soldier's Joy," "Arkansas Traveler," "Mississippi Sawyer," or "White Cockade." He might also have tried his hand at hornpipes like "Ricketts Hornpipe" or "Fishers Hornpipe."

Alice Lloyd College

*"If you run your spring cart over a rough road,
all the small potatoes will go to the bottom."* (1876)

NAILS

Although it's now hard for us to imagine building a house without nails, cabins built before about 1800 seldom used nails, or anything metal, for that matter. For these early cabins, even the door hinges were made out of wood or leather. Before cut nails were invented in 1790, all nails had to be hand forged. In fact, nails were so rare and valuable on the frontier that when a settler abandoned his old cabin to move on to a new place, he would sometimes burn his old cabin to the ground just to extract the nails. Incredibly, there was even an early Virginia law that required an abandoned house to be burned to salvage the precious nails. Only when nails began to be mass produced did they become cheap enough to be purchased by the log cabin pioneer.

OUR CABIN

Library of Congress

Pioneer Insult
"Her tongue is tied in the middle and loose at both ends."

BUILDING THE ROOF

Once the cabin walls were up and the last notes of the fiddle had faded away, most of the merry makers who came for the house raising loaded up their wagons and went home to take care of their livestock and pets. The pioneer himself was left with the task of putting on the roof and finishing the cabin. With the help of his family or a few close neighbors, the roof could be put on in fairly short order.

Mars Hill College

When nails were not even a gleam in a carpenter's eye, the roofs of the earliest cabins could be built using only an axe. The gable side of the roof was built up using proportionally smaller and smaller logs to gain the proper pitch. Starting with what was called a butting pole on the lower end, horizontal ribs were added as the roof gained height. Wooden shakes or clapboards were then laid on top of the ribs and held in place by weight-poles. The entire roof was held in place only by the force of gravity.

When augers and nails became available, roofs were then constructed using rafters held together by wooden pins or nails. Long roof timbers, which were called "purlins," were laid crosswise to the rafters. If nails were available, the purlins would be nailed to the rafters. Otherwise, purlins were attached using leather strips or rope.

"If a husband sits on the roof of his cottage near the chimney for seven hours his next child will be a boy."[29]

CLAPBOARDS

P ioneers in places like Nebraska, where trees were few and far between, often used sod to cover their log houses. Most pioneers, however, favored wooden shakes or clapboards. The common woods used for clapboards were white oak, red oak, chestnut, pine, cedar and occasionally yellow poplar. Oak was a favorite because it was tough, and chestnut and cedar were sometimes used because they resisted rot and insects. Tall, straight-grained trees that were three or four feet in diameter were carefully selected.

> *With a good helper, one clapboard man was said to have turned out 2000 shakes in one day.*

University of Louisville

"Idleness is the devil's workshop."

THE FROE & MAUL

Many early shakes were made using an axe and wooden wedges, which were called "gluts." This changed with the introduction of two tools: the froe and the wooden maul. The froe was formed by a blacksmith using an iron bar that was doubled over to form an eye for the handle. It was sharpened only on one side and was hit with a wooden maul on the other. The froe worked best when it had a dull edge that would split the wood along the grain, rather than cut it. The maul was made so it could be used with one hand, like a hammer. It was cut out of a small tree and baked next to the fireplace with a good, hot fire. Then it was air dried in the shed.

Photo by William Barnhill, Mars Hill College

Uncle Bill O'Kelly, Mount Pisgah, NC

The log that would be used to make clapboards was cut into 2, 3 or 4' sections. Then the froe was placed along the grain in the middle of the end of a section and driven into the log with the wooden maul. The sections were then split into quarters and then into eighths. The heart was split out and used for firewood. The remaining part was ready to be made into boards. The sections were halved until the shakes were the proper thickness.[1]

Roof Lore
Split and put up your shakes in the dark of the moon. Shakes put up on the increase of the moon will cup or warp.

WINDOWLESS CABINS (CONT.)

Many of the earliest cabins were first built without windows. These cabins were often meant to provide only temporary shelter, so windows were thought of as an unnecessary luxury. Since many of these early cabins were unchinked, some sunlight did manage to filter in between the logs. In fact, when Frederick Law Olmstead passed through the South in 1856, he observed that, "Through the chinks as you pass along the road you may often see all that is going on in the house; and, at night, the light of the fire shines brightly out on all sides."[55]

North Carolina Archives & History

Two farmers had swapped mules, but both were grumbling that they thought they'd been cheated. Somebody asked one of the unhappy farmers why he didn't try to get the other farmer to swap back. "Because," said the farmer, "he might try to skin me again."[41]

WINDOWLESS CABINS

After a family had settled into their new cabin, they started thinking about adding a few windows. Since glass was not readily available until the early 1800's, most of the early windows were protected from storms by wooden shutters, or were covered with deer skin scrapped thin or by paper soaked in bear grease. Even when glass did become available, it was often too costly to afford and too fragile to transport over rough roads.

The main reason that most of the early cabins had few, if any, windows was that pioneers spent most of their time outside. Except in rainy weather, for meals and for sleeping, life was lived outside. Another advantage of a windowless cabin was that it provided more protection against Indian attacks in the earliest days of the frontier.

One old tale tells of a small boy who noticed a cabin with windows that were covered with paper smeared with bear grease. "Look, Granny, come see a house with specs on."[13]

University of Louisville

Pioneer Insult: *"He's all vine and no 'taters."*

CHINKING & DAUBING

When early settlers finished building their temporary cabins, they rarely bothered to fill the space between the logs. More important tasks awaited them, like putting food on the table. There was land to clear, gardens to plant and wild game to hunt.

After they had built a more permanent log cabin, most pioneers eventually "chinked." "Chinking" means filling the space between the logs with sticks, bark, wooden wedges, rocks, moss, or practically anything that could be used to stop the flow of air into the cabin. When nails were readily available, some log cabin builders drove nails in between the logs to hold the next layer, which was called "daubing." "Daubing" was a mixture that often included clay and straw with a healthy dose of cow manure added for good measure.

The Old Crawford Place

When it came time to rechink my own cabin, the Old Crawford Place, I found everyone I talked with and every book I read had a different idea about the proper recipe for a good daubing mixture. To learn how the locals in Big Pine, North Carolina chinked and daubed, I consulted with my banjo-pickin' friend and neighbor Jake Owens, who lives nearby in a log cabin he built with his father, fiddler Malcolm Owen. Jake's advice was good as gold: "Make your daubing mixture the consistency of dog s- - t ."

"Bread and company spoil after three days."

THE CHINK-EATING COW

Faced with the task of chinking my own cabin, I wondered what recipe was originally used in daubing the cabin. When I looked between the logs, I could readily see sticks, various pieces of wood, rocks and rusty nails that had been driven in between the logs. I was puzzled as to why the mud daubing was gone from between the lower logs, but fully intact between the upper logs.

Mars Hill College

The answer came from the previous owner, who rechinked the cabin when he lived there in the mid 1970's. He admitted that he used an old daubing recipe that included salt in the mixture. Big mistake! He allowed one of his neighbors to pasture cattle on the property. Hungry for salt, the cattle licked out every bit of the daubing between the logs they could reach. They even climbed up on the porch to get to the delicious salt morsels there and, in the process, broke the porch all to pieces.

After I became friends with the neighbor whose cows had dined on my cabin, I teased him about his "chink-eating cows." I even accused him of eating part of my cabin himself, because he probably ate some of the cattle that had chewed on my cabin. He laughed and denied eating any of those cows, but when I see him, I can't help but think that inside him, somewhere, is part of my cabin. "Give it back!"

"It's not necessary to drink up the whole puddle to find that the water is dirty." (1876)

CABIN WALLS

o two old-timers seem to agree on the perfect way to daub and chink a log cabin. This lack of consensus was probably due to the fact that none ᴄᴏ the methods worked that well. Chinking, it seemed, was not something you did once and forgot about. Instead, it was a constant process of filling in where the chinking fell (or was licked!) out. Adding to the problem was the fact that, as they seasoned and dried out, logs tended to shrink. In wet weather, the logs would expand. Either way, the chinking and daubing had a tough time making a good seal between the logs.

Early pioneers often attached animal skins to the walls to add a layer of insulation, and to cover up cracks where the chinking or daubing fell out. A typical cabin might display the skins of bears, wildcats, coons, skunks and even minks. These stretched skins were not only a shield to keep the cold wind out, they were also a trophy of a good hunt and a logical place for a skin to cure. Horns and antlers were commonly used on inside cabin walls as racks for powder horns, tomahawks, axes and muskets.[13]

Photo by Wayne Erbsen

"Hard work may not kill, but it scares some half to death."

LOG CABIN WALLPAPER

Though the menfolk preferred to line the inside walls of their cabins with skins as proof of past hunting glories, women much preferred something more civilized that was closer to genuine wallpaper. Lacking store bought wallpaper, most women substituted whatever they had, like old feed sacks or anything made of paper, such as magazines and newspapers. In the 1850's, the favorite newspaper used to paper the walls of Western cabins was the *New York Tribune.* It was this newspaper's tantalizing stories about the West that lured pioneers to leave the safety and security of their eastern homes and head west in Conestoga wagons. Horace Greeley, the editor of *The New York Tribune,* was the man who was falsely given credit for the phrase, "Go West young man."

University of North Carolina at Chapel Hill

A Hunting Tale

While out hunting, a mountain man shot a turkey. As it was falling, the turkey hit and killed a deer. The impact knocked the deer's horns into a tree which was loaded with honey. To keep all the honey from flowing out, the hunter grabbed a handful of leaves. Hiding in the leaves was a rabbit. The hunter was so startled, that he hurled the rabbit into the creek. The rabbit landed on several large trout, which were knocked senseless. The hunter then walked over and scooped the trout up in his hat.

MAMA'S NEW WALLPAPER

"Each year Mama applied a new layer of newspapers or magazines to the inside walls of our cabin. She carefully saved back any printed matter she had for just such a purpose. Since reading materials were scarce, she always carefully guarded such treasures. If she had a Sears & Roebuck catalog, sometimes she'd paper the walls with pages from this 'wish book.' On a rainy day, we often sat inside staring at those pages glued up on the walls, pretending we had the money to order just about anything we took a fancy to. We often had to hold up a lantern or a lighted pine splinter to read the words, but we could be entertained for hours just by looking at the pictures."

"Our 'wallpaper' was put up partly to help keep out snakes and bugs, but to me, it just seemed to give the varmints more to chew on. It did seem to slow down the wind from blowing through the cracks on a windy day. The random collage of newspapers gave a cheery yet cluttered look to the cabin. Sometimes it was all we had to read, except the Bible."

University of North Carolina at Chapel Hill

"Nothing rattles like an empty wagon."

ADDING A SHED KITCHEN

The first addition to the original log cabin was always a shed kitchen, which was built out of sawmill lumber rather than logs. Before pioneer women had a separate kitchen of their own, they mainly did the cooking bending over an open hearth. Although the thought of hearth cooking is picturesque from our viewpoint in the 21st century, for pioneer women, it was backbreaking work. To these tired housewives, the idea of standing up over a real cookstove must have seemed like heaven on earth!

Berea College

Don't Blame the Pig

An old farmer and his wife were getting ready to celebrate their 50th wedding anniversary. As family and friends started to arrive, the old lady told her husband, "John, you never slaughtered the hog. Go out there and kill it so we can have some meat!" The old man's face turned sour and he said, "Look, woman. There's no use to blame the pig for something that happened so long ago."[41]

SAWMILLS & SIDING

Mars Hill College

Even as railroads began penetrating the isolated lives of the log cabin pioneers after the Civil War, local sawmills began springing up everywhere. With milled lumber suddenly available, the pioneer now had the luxury of choosing which building materials he wanted to use. Gone were the days when logs were his only choice. For those whose families had outgrown their one room log cabin, here was a chance to enlarge their home at a modest price with materials that were easier to use.

Many log cabin pioneers took advantage of the new availability of whipsawn lumber by covering their cabins with clapboard siding. To them, concealing the logs under freshly painted siding was a big step toward middle-class respectability. With siding, their humble log cabin now closely resembled a real frame house. When we drive down a country road, we can only guess at the historic log cabins that lay hidden under clapboard siding.

Even though the symbol of the log cabin helped to elect Presidents and sold everything from patent medicines to pancake syrup, many pioneers were glad to shed its negative image. After their new frame house was completed, their abandoned cabin either stood as an empty reminder of the old ways, or was turned into a barn or storage shed.

"A hungry rooster keeps quiet when he finds a worm."

MY FIRST PUNCHEONS (CONT.)

L ike many of the skills learned on the frontier, my own lesson in splitting puncheons (split logs) was done the hard way, through hands-on experience and making mistakes. Big ones.

Since the front steps of our cabin were fully rotten, it was time to build a new set of steps. Although I had seen factory-made risers for making steps at the lumber yard, I knew that was not the way to go. Anyway, I never was one to do things the easy way. Instead, my vision was to combine the fine art of hewing with the skill of splitting a log, two essential skills I relished learning.

"It couldn't be all that hard to split a log in half," I told myself. After all, I'd been pretty handy with an axe, a wedge, and a sledgehammer since I was about ten years old. Of course, I used these tools only for splitting firewood.

For starters, I knew I had to pick out a good straight tree. Since I had neither a horse nor oxen, I needed to find a tree that was relatively close to the front of the cabin, because it would have to be dragged by brute force (mine). After scouting out possible trees, I found a nice straight one that was already down. "Ah ha," I thought. "The wind brought this one down, so half the work's done. No problem." The tree was lying not too far from the cabin, up on the hill. "I can roll this baby down the hill after I'm done splitting it." Again, no problem.

I grabbed my saw, two or three iron wedges, an axe and a sledgehammer. "Boy, I was loaded for bear. Look out tree!" The first thing I did was clear away some underbrush so I could work easier. After measuring 45", the length I wanted for my front steps, I cut several lengths out of that

"An ounce of experience is worth a pound of theory."

MY FIRST PUNCHEONS (CONT.)

log. The chips of white wood fell like snow to the ground, and I thought, "Piece of cake!" I did wonder what kind of tree it was, but I couldn't tell for sure. I knew it wasn't a pine or poplar, and it was too soft to be an oak, ash, or walnut. Maybe it was some kind of a gum tree.

Working from one end and then the other, I got my wedges in the wood and was pounding them in with the sledge. But like quicksand, my wedges were sinking deeper and deeper into the wood, but no "splitting" was taking place. The wood was basically sucking in my wedges.

When all three of my wedges were hopelessly buried inside the log, I turned it on its side and frantically began chopping at the faultline with my axe, trying desperately to free my wedges and divide the log in half. After toiling away for what seemed like forever, I finally freed up my wedges, but the crosswise grain was still holding on for dear life, and I thought I'd never get it separated. Covered with sweat and wood chips from head to toe, it was about then that I realized that what

Photo by Janet Swell

Wayne Erbsen at the Old Crawford Place

seemed like a perfectly straight log to begin with was bedeviled with grain that was actually twisted. The two separated halves of my log were hopelessly warped and misshapened. There would be no using these, except for firewood.

"Don't put yourself in a pucker." (1825)

MY FIRST PUNCHEONS

I later found an old, dead red oak tree that had blown over in a storm. After being cut into the proper length, it split in half almost like butter. In only a few minutes, I had two matched halves, perfect for making puncheon

Photo by Wayne Erbsen

steps. This I did with my antique broad axe and a little help from my friend David Jacobs.

The lesson learned? Choose your wood very carefully. Just because a tree "looks" straight on the outside, don't assume the grain is straight on the inside. The type of tree will tell you more about the shape of the grain than what it looks like on the outside. And above all, don't try splitting a gum tree!

Puncheon Time

Before clocks or watches were common, pioneers depended on the position of the sun to tell them the approximate time. When a visitor came carrying a watch, a notch was sometimes made on the floor to mark where the sun had hit at a certain time. One Louisiana woman was once asked the time by a visiting relative. She walked across the room to her sun mark and answered right back, "It's a puncheon and a half before twelve o'clock."[10]

Pioneer Insult
"He's so lazy he won't even scratch when he's got poison ivy."

TALE OF AN OUTHOUSE

Many modern people have to stifle a snicker when they even hear the word "outhouse." 'Course, if they have to "go," and it's the only bathroom around, they don't think it's so dern funny then.

Although I didn't grow up with an outhouse, in the mid-1970's I did manage to experience its many joys when I lived for a short time in an old farmhouse in the mountains of Southwest Virginia, near Volney. On a rare trip to the nearest town of Independence, I had a nice chat with one of the locals, who asked me about the old farm where I was living. "Is your bathroom regular or newfangled?" he asked. I thought for a second and then proudly said, "It's regular." He grinned, and I knew I was a member of the club.

Even before we closed the deal on purchasing the Old Crawford Place, it was clear that I'd have to build an outhouse. "Going" in the woods soon lost its romance. We never did find signs of there being an old outhouse around the place, so it would soon be time to build one.

The biggest thing I'd ever built was a bird house, so here was my chance to roll up my sleeves and actually build a genuine structure. I was pawing the ground with anticipation. Of course, being a college-educated city slicker, I went to the library and wrapped my eyes around a big stack of books on outhouses, both new and old. Some went into the nostalgia of old outhouses, and a few even gave plans for building one. I was soon armed to the teeth and raring to go.

"It's a strange world. People used to eat inside and go to the bathroom outside. Now they eat outside and go to the bathroom inside."
Crawford Worley

CONFESSIONS OF AN OUTHOUSE DIGGER

I knew that the hole itself had to be dug about half way to China, so I got a bright idea. Just the day before, I had hired an experienced backhoe man to begin putting in a road where the old one had once been. While he was there with his heavy equipment, surely he would dig a  little outhouse hole for me. I asked him, and in his pure mountain accent, he assured me he could do the job.

Though it sounded like a fine idea at the time, having the backhoe dig the outhouse hole turned out to be a mistake, a BIG one. To dig the hole, the man used the big bucket on his backhoe. Everything went fine until he got down to about four feet deep, when he mopped his brow and announced, "That's all she's gonna do." He explained that he had hit solid rock and that it would take dynamite to go any further. I looked grimly down into the hole and told him nervously that "I could handle things from here."

Names For Outhouses

Backhouse, can, chamber of delight, closet, comfort station, crapper, head, honey bucket, hopper, johnny, johnny house, latrine, little house, necessary room, path, privy, room and a path, shack out back, shanty, sugar shack, shooting gallery, throne, watchamacallit, willy.

CONFESSIONS OF AN OUTHOUSE DIGGER (CONT.)

It was too late to turn back now. I had a gaping hole in the back yard in the only place level enough to build an outhouse, so, come hell or high water, I was bound and determined to build it there. I got down in that hole and started digging. In a few minutes, I found the massive rock that had stopped the backhoe in its tracks. With a pick and shovel, I did manage to break through the big rock and actually got down to around eight feet deep. But I had never worked so hard in my entire life! My wife, Barbara, shouted encouragement as my head sank lower and lower in the hole, as I tunneled my way to China.

With the hole at last deep enough, construction finally began. I soon realized why it was a colossal mistake getting the backhoe to dig the hole. Since the bucket was so wide, it made a hole that was way too big in diameter. All I really needed was a hole not much bigger around than a good-sized watermelon. It just had to be deep. So now, in addition to being a carpenter, I had to be a structural engineer in order to design a building that would span this enormous hole.

Photo by Wayne Erbsen

As I was peering down in the hole, waiting for divine inspiration, my neighbor came over for a visit. Along with my friend David Jacobs, we spanned the hole with several locust trees that I had recently cut down. From there, things went relatively smoothly, at least for an inexperienced carpenter like myself.

"When you call me a hillbilly, you'd better smile." Ernest Tubb

FINAL CONFESSIONS OF AN OUTHOUSE DIGGER

After all the hammering and sawing was done and the basic structure was complete, I realized the job was far from done. The outhouse was built on one of the few flat pieces of ground on our entire 65 acres. Since the building was perched on the edge of a precipice, anyone using the facilities would likely step out the door and immediately plunge down the mountain. With careful attention to where you stepped, you might avoid such a fate during daylight, but what about when one of us makes a midnight journey to the outhouse? I cringed to think of one of my family members or friends stepping off the edge and falling down the mountain.

What was needed, I thought to myself, was a deck, and not just *any* deck. I soon built what must be America's only outhouse with a wrap-around deck. It was magnificent. As I stood back admiring my handiwork, I knew that the only thing my outhouse needed to make it complete was a Sears & Roebuck catalog.

George Washington and the Cherry Tree

Bored to tears, one mountain boy decided he'd liven things up with a practical joke, so he pushed the outhouse over the bank, and down the hill. It wasn't long before his father found him and the boy made a full confession. As his father cut a willow switch and began to apply a correction to the "seat of learning," the boy said, "But Paw, George Washington's pappy didn't whip him when he 'fessed up to cutting down the cherry tree." "Yes," said his father. "But his pappy wasn't sitting up in the cherry tree when it fell."[41]

"A fine cage won't feed the bird." (1876)

THE OUTHOUSE SONG

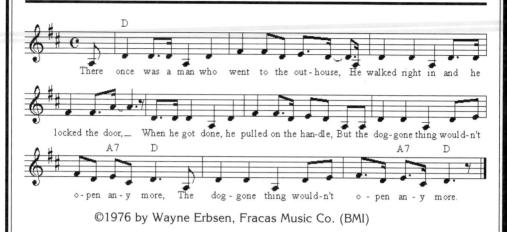

There once was a man who went to the out-house, He walked right in and he locked the door,— When he got done, he pulled on the han-dle, But the dog-gone thing would-n't o-pen an-y more, The dog-gone thing would-n't o-pen an-y more.

He pulled and he tugged and he grabbed that handle,
He pulled on the door with all his might,
The harder he pulled, the longer he stayed there,
'Cuz that old lock had rusted plumb tight,
That old lock had rusted plumb tight.

So he started yellin' for someone to get him,
He screamed and he hollered til his lungs were sore,
There's no one around but one old heffer,
And that old heffer wouldn't open the door,
No, that old heffer wouldn't open the door.

So he started jerkin' and a banging on the ceiling,
He pounded on the walls with all his will,
'Til he jerked that building right off its footings,
And that contraption rolled down the hill,
That contraption rolled down the hill.

It hit the bottom with an awful racket,
And that old lock it lost its grip,
The door flew open, and he started walking,
He'll never forget that awful trip,
He'll never forget that awful trip.

So let this be a farewell warning,
Don't lock the door or if you will,
You might take you an unplanned journey
It's better to walk to the bottom of the hill,
It's better to walk to the bottom of the hill.

THE HOT SEAT

There was nothing worse than having to go out to the outhouse in the middle of winter when the weather was really severe. Even worse than trekking through the ice and snow to get there was knowing how cold the seat would be once you sat down. Some country people used to keep the toilet seat behind the wood cookstove. When they got ready to go to the outhouse, they'd bring the warmed seat with them. Good thinking!

University of North Carolina at Chapel Hill

The editor of a small newspaper noticed that a local farmer's subscription had lapsed. On his way home from work one day, he stopped and chatted with the farmer, who was standing next to his corncrib. "You know," said the editor, "if you're a little short, you can pay for your subscription with two or three bushels of corn." The farmer shrugged and pointed to his empty corn crib. "If I had two or three bushels of corn, I sure wouldn't need your newspaper."

1st Man: *"I'm sorry to hear your bathroom caught fire and burned last night."*

2nd Man: *"Yeah, it was a great loss. I'm just glad the flames didn't touch the house."*

THE FRONTIER FIDDLER

Although some backwoods preachers contemptuously referred to him as "the right hand man to the devil," the frontier fiddler occupied a unique role in pioneer life. A good fiddler was held in the highest esteem, even over preachers, doctors and politicians. Fiddle music was always a key ingredient for any kind of social gathering, such as dances, parties, barn raisings, house warmings, or cornhuskings. Fiddlers were in such high demand that any community that could boast of a good fiddler was the envy of all.

But even though the fiddler was a prized member of a pioneer community, there was always a dark cloud that hung over him. He was plagued by the centuries-old notion that "the devil rides the fiddle bow." Anyone playing "the devil's box" was accused of "doing the devil's handiwork." Fire-and-brimstone preachers were fond of calling fiddlers "Lieutenants of Hell," and even today, you hear the expression "Thick as fiddlers in Hell."

Frontier fiddlers added to their own unsavory reputation when they mixed music with whiskey. In some rural communities, it was common for the fiddler to be paid in moonshine. Even his choice of tunes reflects not only his penchant for strong drink, but his association with the devil: "Give the Fiddler a Dram," "Fiddler's Drunk and the Fun's All Over," "Devil in the Strawstack," "Devil's Dream," "Hell up Cole Holler," and "Devil in the Woodpile."

The fiddler's curious practice of keeping a rattlesnake rattle inside his fiddle didn't help his reputation, either. Many fiddlers swore that the rattle improved the tone of their instrument, while others said it merely kept spiders from building webs inside their fiddles. Either way, fiddlers and serpents were indelibly intertwined for those with suspicious minds.

LEARNING THE FIDDLE FROM THE DEVIL HIMSELF

"If you want to play a fiddle, go on a dark night at twelve o'clock to the forks of a road. Sit down with your fiddle over your shoulder just like you were going to play. While you are sitting there, a big black snake will crawl by you with his head up in the air. Don't get scared. The snake will go up the road and turn around and a big black man with a fiddle will come back down the road and stand by you and play three or four pieces on his fiddle. Then he will disappear and you can go home and play any piece on the fiddle you want. I knew a man in Missouri that done this, and he was the best player in the state on a fiddle."[5]

State Historical Society of Wisconsin

> *"Before sunrise for five mornings, take a fiddle and go into the country 'til you come to the end of one of the main roads or to a cross-roads, and on the fifth morning you will meet a man also carrying a fiddle. He will teach you to play. He is the devil."*[57]

Pioneer Insult: *"He was drunk as a fiddler's clerk."*

FIDDLIN' DAVY CROCKETT

Among the early well-known frontier fiddlers was Davy Crockett. Though he claimed he was "half-horse, half-alligator, and a little touched with snapping turtle," he was actually a fine fiddler and a buckdancer. His tune "Colonel Crockett's Reel" was collected as early as 1839, and is still played in West Virginia under the title, "The Route."[57]

Great Smoky National Park

Davy Dancing

With Indians watching in disbelief, Davy Crockett once danced a breakdown on a great flat rock with such vigor that, "The old rock began to snap and smoke like a hemlock backlog; and when his dancing caused sparks that set fire to the Indian blankets, he did a 'Grind the Bottle' to stomp out the fire."[18]

"What's the difference between a fiddle and a violin?"
"About five dollars."

THOMAS JEFFERSON, FIDDLER

Besides being the third president of the United States and the author of the Declaration of Independence, Thomas Jefferson was one of the first great violinists in colonial America. In his early years, he played the violin every day, sometimes practicing up to three hours. Even when traveling overseas as a diplomat, he carried a small violin with him. In 1786, while in France on a diplomatic mission, Jefferson fell and badly injured his right wrist. The bone was poorly set, and he was left with a wrist that was permanently stiff. This painful injury eventually made Jefferson give up playing the violin. In his will he gave his prized violin, an Amaiti dated 1660, to one of his slaves.

Fiddles & the Church

Because of the strong influence of the church in frontier life, many fiddlers quit playing the fiddle when they joined the church. Many a newly saved fiddler burned up his fiddle or busted it to pieces by hitting it against a stout tree. Some fiddlers may have quit playing but were reluctant to destroy their instruments. You occasionally hear stories of someone who takes apart an old log cabin only to find a fiddle hidden behind the walls. Apparently, some fiddlers quit playing but couldn't bear to destroy their instrument, so they hid it behind a wall in the hope that someday it would be found and played again.

University of North Carolina at Chapel Hill

FIDDLIN' BILL HENSLEY

Typical of the Southern mountain musicians was Fiddlin' Bill Hensley. Born near Johnson City, Tennessee in about 1870, he claimed to have walked barefooted across the mountains when his family moved to the Big Laurel section of Madison County, North Carolina. He acquired a fiddle when his father swapped 20 acres of land for a hog rifle and an old fiddle that had gone through the Civil War. When he joined the army to fight in the Spanish-American War, Bill even took his fiddle, which he used to entertain his fellow soldiers while stationed in the Philippines.

Library of Congress

Fiddlin' Bill later moved to Avery Creek, North Carolina, where he purchased 220 acres of mountain land. At the ripe old age of 68, he cleared eight acres and built a four room log cabin along with a barn and put in a big garden. There he lived with his wife, who was also nicknamed "Bill."

When he was 75 years of age, Fiddlin' Bill got into a drunken gun battle with Clarence Harwood, 24, of Avery's Creek, North Carolina. Harwood was killed, and Fiddlin' Bill was sentenced to 2-3 years at Raleigh's Central Prison. Fiddlin' Bill even brought his fiddle to prison, and he was invited by the warden to play for the prisoners in the yard.

"Don't stop stirrin' 'til the puddin's done." (1834)

THE VIRGINIA REEL
ACCORDING TO MARK TWAIN

"**T**he dancers are formed in two long ranks, facing each other, and the battle opens with some light skirmishing between the pickets, which is gradually resolved into a general engagement along the whole line; after that you have nothing to do but stand by and grab every lady that drifts within reach of you, and swing her. It is very entertaining, and elaborately scientific also."[4] (1863)

"The man who can fiddle all through one of those Virginia Reels without losing his grip, may be depended upon in any kind of musical emergency."   Mark Twain

Mars Hill College

Fiddlin' Bill Hensley's Tunes

Sourwood Mountain, Bonapart's Retreat, Last Gold Dollar, Old Granny Rattletrap, Jenny Put the Kettle On, Grey Eagle, Black-Eyed Susie, Hoppin' Lulu, Rickett's Hornpipe, Cumberland Gap, Buckin' Mule, Cripple Creek, Patty on the Turnpike, Turkey in the Straw, Soldier's Joy, Lady Hamilton, Old Joe Clark, Ida Red, Sally Gooden, Ol' Booger Man, Squallin' Cat.[2]

BARN DANCES (CONT.)

When the building of a log cabin was complete, a dance was always held. Known as "barn dances" or "frolics," they often took place in the newly-completed cabin, but just as often were held in a barn, a schoolhouse, or in a clearing in the woods. While some of the untrained dancers were often rough and un-couth, others were "smooth enough to dance on a window-glass without breaking it."[18] One observer saw "Buck-toothed, heavily-shod males dragging giggling straggly-haired and blushing gals around in a continuous whirl that would have made even the solar system dizzy."[7]

Musicians (l to rt.) J.C. McCool, Walter Davis, Clarence Greene

Fiddlers at such dances were known to have played such tunes as "Cotton-Eyed Joe," "The Downfall of Paris," and the "Flowers of Edinburgh."[2] While they were fiddling, many had to dodge flying elbows and exuberant kicks. With the addition of corn whiskey, some dances turned violent and musicians even had to dodge stray bullets.

"Don't stand in the sun if you have butter on your head."

BARN DANCES

Aunt Jennie Wilson, from West Virginia, remembered playing banjo at some barn dances in her youth:

"I've really seen some skirmishes at dances, I'll tell you. One night someone fired a pistol and the shot went through my banjer and I thought for sure I was shot. I remember many a time I would go to a dance carrying a pistol when I was just a girl."[28]

Photo by Eilleen Gardner Galer

Old-Time Dances

Diggin' Potatoes, Dog Scratch, Railing Twist, Tennessee Stomp, Broke-Legged Mule, Hen Waller, Breakin' the Cow's Neck, Walkin' the Grapevine, Dog Hop, Double Shuffle, Goin' to Talk to the Judge, Walkin' the Puncheons, Headin' the Steer, Train a-Puffin', Makin' up Bread, Rabbit Hop, Rockin' the Cradle, Crow Hop, Big Apple, Cleanin' the Bottoms of Your Shoes, Whipstitch, Threadin' the Needle, Rockin' the Cradle, Shine the Shoes.[18]

"You may talk of your bar hunts, your deer hunts, and your knottin' tigers' tails through the bung-holes of barrels, but if a regular-built frolic don't beat 'em all blind for fun, then I'm no judge of fun, that's all!"
George Washington Harris (1845).[18]

"Better a lame donkey than no horse." (1854)

OLD HICKORY'S FANDANGO

I n Virginia there lived an old planter by the name of Major Hanley. Some considered him odd; others thought him quite crazy. Either way, he made it a rule to play a practical joke on everyone he met.

Hanley got his chance one chilly, drizzly evening when a lone horseman unwittingly arrived at his door. The stranger had lost his way, and as was the custom of the day, requested to spend the night. With Southern hospitality, a servant brought him into the living room where Hanley welcomed him to warm himself by a roaring fire in the fireplace. Directly, supper was announced, and the two sat down to the pleasantries of a hearty meal.

When they had finished their supper, Hanley got up and graciously excused himself from the table. He returned in a few minutes carrying what was described as a "large horse-pistol." Walking nervously behind Hanley was one of his servants carrying a fiddle and a bow. Hanley bowed deeply and then said, "My dear friend. We must not let the evening pass without a little amusement. From your looks I know you can dance. So, Sir, you will take your place upon the floor and dance us a reel. You look like a Scotsman, so come, make no delay."

Protesting that he had not danced since boyhood, the guest was immediately shown the business end of Hanley's pistol. He danced. Even with his heavy boots, the guest reluctantly danced around the room to the wretched squawking of the servant's fiddle. The fiddling was so bad that Hanley threatened to shoot his servant if his fiddling did not soon improve.

Finally, the tired guest sat down and declared he was done dancing. Before Hanley could order him back on the floor, he was distracted by the sounds of a horse approaching the house. Hanley absentmindedly laid the pistol on the table and left the room. The guest immediately grabbed the pistol and, as he half-suspected, found it to be unloaded. With his own powder and ball, he expertly loaded the weapon.

When Hanley returned, he looked for his pistol, but found it in the hands of his guest. "The pistol is now loaded, Sir, by my own powder flask and ball flask. We will continue the amusement by a dance executed by the master of the house. And let me assure you I can use a pistol much better than I can dance a reel. Dance, Sir, or I'll put a bullet through your legs, if not through your heart."

It was Hanley's turn to dance, and dance he did. More than once he requested to stop, but the guest urged him on with a wave of the pistol. Finally, to disarm the weapon, the guest fired the pistol up the chimney, and Hanley sat down, both relieved and quite out of breath. His servant then went over and whispered in Hanley's ear what he had found out while Hanley was absent from the room. The guest, he swore, was none other than General Andrew Jackson, Old Hickory himself!

Hanley's tone changed rapidly when he found out the name of his honored guest. The two men soon shook hands and enjoyed a laugh and a drink together. History didn't record if this episode quenched Hanley's thirst for practical jokes, but we can guess that, at least, it slowed it down some![57]

For log cabin pioneers, singing was not something that was only done by a chosen few on a Saturday night. Instead, virtually everyone sang, and it didn't matter if it was during the day or the night, or both. To those of us living in the 21st century, this notion that everyone sang must indeed seem strange. Somehow, somewhere, we have been taught to believe that singing should be reserved for special occasions and done only by people with "good voices." Anyone not possessing this "good voice" must endure the jokes, the snickers and even the ridicule of those around them, until they learn to confine their singing to the privacy of their own shower.

"The family sang line by line."

More and more, instead of remaining active participants in music, we have merely become passive consumers. We buy our music at the store; we rent videos, and we pay to attend concerts. We've come to idolize "professionals," while our own talents go unrealized and unrewarded. Most people, in fact, have a downright inferiority complex when it comes to singing. Given the choice between standing on a stage and singing to a crowd of people or running buck naked through a crowded city park in broad daylight, most folks would choose the park.

"If you like music, get married and play second fiddle."

LOG CABIN SINGING (CONT.)

Our modern attitudes toward singing are in stark contrast to those of log cabin pioneers. To them, singing was as natural as talking, as breathing. Young and old all sang. Sometimes families sang hymns together around the hearthside or piano. But most singing was done by individuals as they went about their daily lives. Kids sang songs in school, and the girls always sang jump-rope rhymes during recess. Farmers sang while they plowed, worked in the fields or mended fences. Women sang while performing their daily chores. For these women, singing was not just to pass the time, but was also a way to let their young children know where to find them in the house or in the yard.

Jim Bollman Collection

In early pioneer days when instruments were rare, people sang because it was the only music they had. But even after instruments became common, a strong singing tradition continued. It was the women who tended to do more of the singing, while the menfolk played the instruments. This was partially due to pioneer attitudes. Instruments like the fiddle or the banjo were widely associated with the devil. The "proper" instrument for a woman was the piano, the dulcimer, the guitar or the zither. A woman's main "instrument" was her voice. Many women knew hundreds of songs by heart and took pride in being able to remember all the verses of ballads like "Barbary Allen."

LOG CABIN SINGING (CONT.)

Children learned to sing as early as they learned to talk. The songs they sang were learned from their mothers or from other children. Even as these children grew into young adults, there was no division between the songs sung by adults and those sung by the younger generation. Now, of course, it's a whole new kettle of fish! Deep divisions exist between the music of the different generations. These differences are highlighted by the entertainment industry, which profits because it has more markets to sell to. It is well to remember that in pioneer days, there was but one type of music, and it was enjoyed by young and old alike.

Alice Lloyd College

Learning music in pioneer days usually meant remembering the songs heard around home. Except for an occasional hymnal, there were no songbooks. Sheet music was so rare that it was likely to end up as wallpaper!

Because songs were sung from memory, they often changed with countless singings. The name of the composer was long forgotten, and songs were

Popular Pioneer Ballads

Barbara Allen, The Golden Vanity, Gypsy Laddie, Geordie, False Knight on the Road, John Riley, Butcher Boy, Early in the Spring, Wagoner's Lad, Fair and Tender Ladies, Two Sisters, Lord Bateman, Wife of Usher's Well, Lord Thomas & Fair Ellinor.[48]

LOG CABIN SINGING

shaped by the many singers who sang them. The evolution of these folk songs eventually ended when collectors began committing the old songs to paper. Instead of being free to change, the songs were now frozen in time. The new singers who bought these song collections tended to sing them the way they found them in the books. Although this certainly helped preserve songs that might otherwise be lost, it ended their gradual evolution.

Despite the fact that practically everyone sang, the number of new songs that were added to the pioneer's repertoire were actually quite few. This was because log cabin culture relished the old over the new. Singers were rewarded with approval when they remembered an old song, not when they created a new one. For those who did compose new songs, they often apologized for it.

In the evening, after chores were done, pioneers made time for music. In the summer, music was often played on the front porch, and in wintertime, it might happen at the hearth in front of a blazing fire. Evening was the time when the scariest ghost stories were told, the longest ballads were sung, and the best banjo and fiddle tunes were played.

Georgia Department of Archives & History

"A dog can't bark and bite at the same time."

SINGING SCHOOLS (CONT.)

To get more people to sing hymns in church, singing schools were held in backwoods communities by traveling singing-school masters. By the early 1800's, these masters, often traveling by mule or wagon, visited remote pioneer settlements to teach the rudiments of a "newfangled" style of reading notes that was known as "shape-note singing." The idea was to give each do, re or mi of the scale a characteristic shape. Once singers learned to recognize the shapes and associate them with their relative pitch on the scale, whole congregations could be led through complicated hymns in fairly short order.

There was always an air of excitement on the first night of singing school, which might have been held in a church or one-room school house. With sweat dripping off his brow, the singing master could be seen lugging in an armload of songbooks, a chart showing the musical symbols and a carpet-bag of his tools - a tuning fork, tablets and pencils, a baton, and maybe a handkerchief to mop his brow.

As candles and lanterns flickered, the students sat in a semi-circle two or three rows deep, while the master taught them their shapes. They soon learned to sing in three or four parts, while keeping the beat with an up and down motion of their right hand. When the master was satisfied his students could "sing the paint off a barn door," the class held an open recital for family and friends. The singing-school master then climbed back on his mule and headed down the road in search of another group of willing students.

SINGING SCHOOLS

Though these singing schools were quite popular, some scoffers looked down their noses at what they called "buckwheat notes," "patent notes," or "three-cornered sounds." Such name calling only instilled in shape-note singers a deeper determination to keep singing the shapes. They defiantly called their detractors "Round Heads," after the round notes they used.

Although shape-note singing had largely disappeared, singing conventions using such books as *The Christian Harmony* are still occasionally held in rural Southern communities. But even though the booming voices of the singing school masters have long faded away, they have left an indelible mark on American music. The harmony singing we hear today owes a debt to these masters, who braved the backwoods roads to teach rural settlers their do-re-mis.

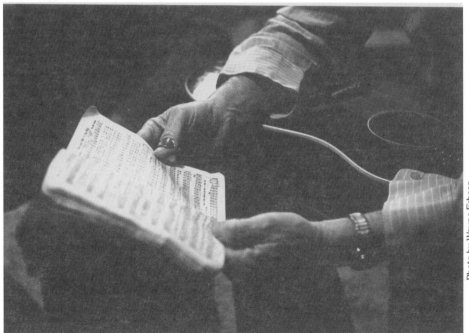

"Dry bread at home is better'n roast meat an' gravy abroad." (1868)

BARBARA ALLEN

No other English ballad even comes close to the popularity of "Barbara Allen." Brought over by the earliest pioneers, its roots can be traced back at least to the year 1666. As a boy, Abraham Lincoln sang "Barbara Allen" while growing up in Indiana.

'Twas in the mer - ry month of May, When all gay flowers were bloom-ing, Sweet Wil - liam on his death-bed lay, For the love of Barb-ara Al-len.

He sent his servant to the town
He sent him to her dwelling
Saying; Master's sick and very sick,
And for your sake he's dying.

Slowly, slowly, she gets up
And to his bedside going
She drew the curtains to one side
And says: Young man, you're dying.

He reached out his pale, white hands
Intending for to touch her
She jumped, she skipped all over the room
And says: Young man, I won't have you.

He turned his pale face to the wall
And bursted out a-crying
Saying: Adieu to thee, adieu to all
Adieu to Barbara Allen.

She had not more than reached the town
She heard the death bells tolling
She looked to the east, she looked to the west
And saw his pale face coming.

"Fair words butter no parsnips." (1876)

BARBARA ALLEN

Hand down, hand down that corpse of clay
And let me gaze upon him
The more she gazed, the more she grieved
And she bursted out a-crying.

Cursed, cursed, be my name
And cursed be my nature
For this man's life I might have saved
If I had done my duty.

O mother, O mother, go make my bed
And make it long and narrow
Sweet William died for me today
And I'll die for him tomorrow.

Sweet William died on Saturday night
Miss Barbara died on Sunday
The old lady died for the love of both
She died on Easter Monday.

Sweet William was carried to one churchyard
Miss Barbara to another
A briar grew out of one of their graves
A rose tree out of the other.

They grew as high as the old church top
They could not grow any higher
They bound and tied in a true love's knot
For all true lovers to admire.

University of North Carolina at Chapel Hill

"Don't holler 'til you're out of the woods."

THE BLACKEST CROW

Among the ballads collected in the North Carolina mountains in 1916 by English folksong scholar Cecil Sharp was "My Dearest Dear." Carl Sandburg titled it "The Lovers Lament" in his 1927 book, *The American Songbag*. It is also known as "The Time Draws Near." Most people now call it "The Blackest Crow."

As time draws near my dear - est dear when you and I___ must part,

How lit-tle___ you know of the grief and woe In my poor___ ach___ ing heart.

Tis but I suf - fer for your sake be - lieve me dear it's true,

I wish that you were stay - ing here or I was go - ing with you.

I wish my breast was made of glass,
Wherein you might behold
Upon my heart your name lies wrote
In letters made of gold.

> In letters made of gold my love,
> Believe me when I say
> You are the one I will adore
> Until my dying day.

The blackest crow that ever flew,
Would surely turn to white
If ever I proved false to you
Bright day will turn to night.

> Bright day will turn to night my love,
> The elements will mourn
> If ever I prove false to you
> The seas will rage and burn.

ONE TOUGH HOG

T he razorback hog was the toughest animal that ran on four legs. It could take a licking and come back for more.

A farmer was clearing a field of stumps the hard way, by hand. A county extension agent came along and instructed the farmer on the latest device used to clear new ground of stumps: dynamite. Armed with this new knowledge, the farmer went to the general store and purchased dynamite, fuses and blasting caps. When he returned, he set the dynamite in a

University of Louisville

hole he had dug next to a white oak stump and lit the fuse. When the dynamite didn't ignite, the farmer went in the house for supper, forgetting about the dynamite.

The next morning, the farmer's big razorback hog was foraging for its breakfast, found the stick of dynamite and ate it. Still feeling hungry, the hog then went into the barn and brazenly ate out of the mule's feed trough. The mule then rared back and kicked the hog, which, of course, ignited the dynamite. You never heard such an explosion in your life! Hearing the noise, a neighbor rushed over to see what all the commotion was about. When he arrived, the farmer complained, "Just look! The dynamite not only killed my mule, it wrecked the barn, broke every window out of one side of the house and brother, I've got an awful sick hog."[3]

Pioneer Insult
"He would steal acorns from a blind hog." (1851)

DARLING CORY

A proper young pioneer lady would not have been caught dead with the likes of Darling Cory. According to the song, this young hellion made moonshine but drank wine; she packed a .44 but picked a banjo. Any one of these activities would have made her an outcast in frontier times. Women were never known to have made moonshine. Instead, their job seemed to be to discourage their menfolk from making and drinking it. They had little success at doing either. The only other song that paints a picture of another whiskey-making woman is the North Carolina ballad, "Oh Mama, Don't Make Any Liquor Tonight."[5]

As if making moonshine was not bad enough, playing the banjo would have marked Darling Cory as a loose woman. Although a few women did play the banjo and the fiddle, most women were discouraged from doing so as "conduct unbecoming a lady." The banjo and fiddle were considered instruments of the devil and were usually reserved for the rough and rowdy men who drank whiskey and played for dances, which sometimes erupted in violence.

"Darling Cory" was first collected by Cecil Sharp in Burnsville, North Carolina as "The Gambling Man." The first commercial recording of it was by Buell Kazee on April 20, 1927 for Brunswick records. On July 20, 1927, it was also recorded by B.F. Shelton from Corbin, Kentucky for RCA Victor.[31]

In this version, the words are a composite of verses that I have collected from various sources over the past thirty years. The unusual melody is one I learned from Jack Wallen of Sodom Laurel, North Carolina, who learned it from his mother.

Pioneer Insult: *"He stood behind the door too long."*

DARLING CORY

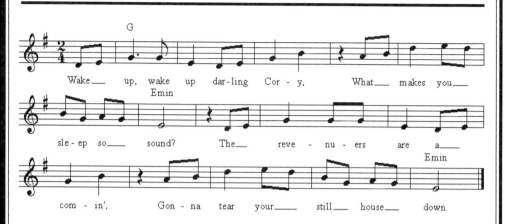

Wake__ up, wake up dar-ling Cor-y, What__ makes you__ sle-ep so__ sound? The__ reve-nu-ers are a__ com-in', Gon-na tear your__ still__ house__ down.

Dig a hole, dig a hole in the meadow,
Dig a hole in the cold, cold ground.
Go and dig you a hole in the meadow,
Gonna lay darling Cory down.

Oh, the first time I saw darling Cory,
She was sitting on the banks of the sea,
With a .44 strapped around her,
And a banjo on her knee. (Chorus)

Don't you hear those bluebirds singing,
Don't you hear their mournful sound?
They're preachin' Cory's funeral,
In some lonesome church yard ground. (Chorus)

Oh the last time I saw darlin' Cory
She had a wine glass in her hand.
She was drinkin' down her troubles,
With a lowdown sorry man. (Chorus)

A modest pioneer woman was asked if she had seen Halley's Comet in 1910. "Yes," she answered, "But only from a distance."[54]

"It's better to be rich and healthy than poor and sick."
John Erbsen

EAST VIRGINIA

The first time I heard the song "East Virginia" was in March or April of 1962. A small but enthusiastic group of us filled the seats in a folk club in West Hollywood, California. Known as the Ash Grove, it was a mecca for hearing grass-roots Southern music, played by the masters. On the stage were four musicians from North Carolina and Tennessee: guitarist Arthel "Doc" Watson, Fiddlin' Fred Price, Clint Howard on guitar and Clarence "Tom" Ashley on banjo. As an audience new to folk music, we didn't quite know what to expect, but we were ready for anything. What we heard simply blew our hats in the creek. Here was the genuine article.

On top of the virtuosity of Doc Watson's blazing guitar playing, I remember being struck with the playing and singing of the banjo player, Tom Ashley. This was the first time I remember seeing anyone play by stroking or hitting down on the strings, a style I later found was known as clawhammer, frailing, framming, or knocking the banjo.

One of my favorite stories about old-time musicians is the tale of how Ashley was "rediscovered." As a young man, Ashley made his living with music by playing banjo, often in blackface, for medicine shows. His job was to draw and entertain a crowd with comedy, songs, skits and old-time banjo pickin'. When Tom had sufficiently warmed up the audience, a "doctor," "Indian," or "professor" would step forward selling snake oil medicine that was guaranteed "to cure what ails you and make you feel like bear hunting armed only with a hickory switch." Eventually, these medicine shows died out, due to changing musical tastes and new laws by the Food and Drug Administration.

"Don't hide your light under a bushel."

Not to be deterred by the demise of the medicine shows, Ashley continued to play for square dances and even showed up with his banjo on pay day at coal mines, where he "busked" for dimes and quarters thrown into a hat.

His music eventually got the attention of record companies like Columbia and RCA Victor, and he recorded a number of songs for those labels. However, the Depression kept a lid on sales, so Ashley pretty much hung up his banjo.

In about 1960, Ashley's early recordings were re-released on a six record set, "The Anthology of American Folk Music." This compilation by Harry Smith had a big impact on the urban folksong revival, which was centered around college campuses in places like New York and California. Among those who heard and were inspired by this anthology was Ralph Rinzler. In the summer of 1960, Rinzler, an ace mandolin player himself, showed up at the Union Grove fiddler's convention in North Carolina. Besides going to play music, Rinzler was on the lookout for some of the older musicians who had made early recordings and then retreated into obscurity.

"If you can't improve on silence, keep silent." (1876)

EAST VIRGINIA (CONT.)

Rinzler approached an old man who was playing a banjo and asked if he'd ever heard of a banjo player named Clarence Ashley. The old man thought for a second and said that he didn't recall such an individual. Rinzler thanked him and started to walk away when the man perked up and said, "Wait a minute! I'm Clarence Ashley." Apparently, he had been using his nickname, Tom, for so long, he forgot his given name was "Clarence."

Blue Ridge Heritage Archives, Ferrum College

The names Tom or Clarence notwithstanding, Ralph Rinzler was excited to have rediscovered this legendary musician. He immediately made plans to return to North Carolina to record Ashley's music for a new audience. True to his word, Rinzler returned with recording equipment and recorded several sessions in Ashley's home. Not only did the tape recorder capture Ashley, but it also helped give recognition to the music of "Doc" Watson, who would soon earn fame as one of the great guitarists of our time.

EAST VIRGINIA

I was born in East Vir-gin-ia North Caro-li-na__ I did__ go, There I met a fair young maid-en__ And her name I__ did not__ know.

Oh her hair was dark in color,
And her lips were ruby red,
On her breast she wore white linen,
There I longed to lay my head.

Papa says we cannot marry,
Mama says it'll never do,
But if you'll only say you love me,
I will run away with you.

I'd rather be in some dark holler,
Where the sun don't ever shine
Than to see you with another,
And to know you'll never be mine.

I'll go back to East Virginia,
North Carolina ain't my home,
I'll go back to East Virginia,
Leave old North Carolina alone.

A country boy went to town to buy an engagement ring for his girlfriend. He was suckered into buying what he thought was a diamond ring with a stone as big as a horse-apple. When he finally got home, he proudly presented it to his girlfriend, who was shocked at its size. "Do you think it's a real diamond?" she asked hopefully. "If it's not," said the boy, "I've been snookered out of two dollars and seventy-five cents."[41]

"Looks won't split rails."

FOUR NIGHTS DRUNK

This hilarious ballad tells of a husband who has arrived home drunk as a skunk and suspects that his wife has been entertaining a suitor. The questions and answers that follow make this one of the most humorous and popular of the old ballads. Also known as "Our Goodman" and "Cabbage Head," it was collected in Scotland as early as 1769. Versions have also been found in France and Germany. In an effort to present this ballad as I have heard it in the Southern mountains, I have included the slang of "ort" for "ought" and "splain" for "explain."

I came in the other night as drunk as I could be, Saw somebody's horse in the stable, where my horse ort to be. "Come here my little wifey, and 'splain this thing to me, Whose horse in the stable where my horse ort to be?"

"You drunk fool, you blind old fool,
    can't you plainly see,
It's nothing but a milk cow my grannie gave to me."
"I've traveled this wide world over, 10,000 miles or more,
But a saddle on a milk cow, I've never seen before."

I came in the other night as drunk as I could be,
Saw somebody's boots in the corner,
    where my boots ort to be.
"Come here my little wifey, and 'splain this thing to me,
Whose boots there in the corner
    where my boots ort to be?"

FOUR NIGHTS DRUNK

"You drunk fool, you blind old fool, can't you plainly see,
It's nothing but a cream jar my granny gave to me."
"I've traveled this wide world over, 10,000 miles or more,
But boot heels on a cream jar, I've never seen before."

I came in the other night as drunk as I could be,
Saw somebody's hat on the hat rack
      where my hat ort to be.
"Come here my little wifey, and 'splain this thing to me,
How come there's a hat on the hat rack
      where my hat ort to be?"
"You drunk fool, you blind old fool, can't you plainly see,
It's only a thunder-jug your grannie gave to me."
"I've traveled this wide world over, 10,000 miles or more,
But a John B. Stetson thunder-jug, I've never seen before."

I came in the other night as drunk as I could be,
Saw a pair of britches, where my britches ort to be.
"Come here my little wifey, and 'splain this thing to me,
How come there's a pair of britches,
      where my britches ort to be."
"You drunk fool, you blind old fool, can't you plainly see,
It's only a dishrag my grannie gave to me."
"I've traveled this wide world over, 10,000 miles or more,
But suspenders on a dishrag, I've never seen before."

I came in the other night as drunk as I could be,
Saw a head on the pillow, where my head ort to be.
"Come here my little wifey, and 'splain this thing to me,
How come there's a head on the pillow,
      where my head ort to be."
"You drunk fool, you blind old fool, can't you plainly see,
It's only a cabbage head my grannie gave to me."
"I've traveled this wide world over, 10,000 miles or more,
But a mustache on a cabbage head, I've never seen before."

"I was happy as if I lived in a gold mansion."
Effie Price, 86, log cabin pioneer

FRANKIE SILVERS (CONT.)

Her real name was Frances Steward Silvers, but they all called her Frankie. The words chiseled into her tombstone give us a chilling reminder of what this story is about: "Frankie Silvers, Only Woman Ever Hanged in Burke County, Morganton, July 2, 1833."

I first heard about this strange chapter of North Carolina folklore from a mountain man named Bobby McMillan, whom I met when I lived in Hickory, North Carolina in the mid-1970's. Because he was the third cousin to Charlie Silvers, the man Frankie was accused of killing, Bobby had been collecting stories, songs and lore about Frankie Silvers since he was a small lad.

The story takes place in what is now Mitchell County, North Carolina, between the Blue Ridge and the Allegheny mountains. It was there, near a branch of the Toe River, that Charlie Silvers built a one-room pole cabin out of round logs. A handsome young man who was just 20-years old, Charlie was known both as a good dancer and also as a good singer. At 19-years old, his wife Frankie was considered a pretty girl and also a good dancer.

Just before Christmas one year, Charlie was getting ready to go hunting up on the Tennessee line. A bad snowstorm was raging, so in order to keep his wife and baby daughter warm while he was gone, Charlie chopped down a hickory tree. After he had split all the wood and stacked it on the porch, Charlie came in covered with ice and snow and laid down in front of the fire to get warm. He took his baby daughter, Nancy, in his arms and soon fell asleep.

This was Frankie's chance to kill Charlie. No one knows why Frankie wanted to murder her husband. Some say it was jealousy, while others say that Charlie was a violent

FRANKIE SILVERS (CONT.)

man who frequently beat Frankie. What is certain is that Frankie took the baby from Charlie's arms and then struck him a blow with the axe as he lay sleeping in front of the fire. After she hit him, he screamed, "God save the child!" She immediately dropped the axe and hid in the bed under the covers. After some time, she heard no sounds, so she came out from under the quilts and found that Charlie was dead.

University of North Carolina at Chapel Hill

That night, Frankie, possibly with the help of her father, cut up Charlie's body with the axe and burned him in the fireplace with the wood that Charlie had cut, split, and stacked on the front porch. They hid the internal organs, which wouldn't burn, in a hollow stump some distance from the cabin.

The next day, Charlie's step-mother, Nancy, and her sisters were washing clothes in an old washpot in the yard when Frankie came walking down the hill with her baby. Frankie told them she had been washing and cleaning her cabin all morning. When asked where Charlie was, Frankie said he had gone across the river on the ice to get his

FRANKIE SILVERS (CONT.)

liquor and had not yet returned. When Charlie didn't show up the next day, Frankie took the baby and went to stay at her father's house. Before she left, she boarded up the door and windows.

Meanwhile, Charlie's father became concerned because his son hadn't come back, so he and a party of men went to nearby Tennessee looking for him. There he found a fortune teller whose conjure ball indicated that Charlie, or his remains, was still in the cabin.

Great Smoky Mountains National Park

"Don't get above your raisin'."

FRANKIE SILVERS (CONT.)

Jake Collis, one of Charlie's friends, was also suspicious that Charlie had been murdered. Accompanied by the Sheriff, Jake went to Charlie's cabin. After prying off the boards that Frankie had nailed over the door and windows, they found the one-room cabin had been scrubbed spotlessly clean. Investigating further, the Sheriff noticed that the ashes in the fireplace looked greasy. He and Jake then raised up the puncheon in front of the fireplace and found blood stains on the dirt, along with teeth and chips of bone. The axe that lay nearby was unusually dull, as if it had been chopping something other than wood.

Just then, Frankie, who had been hiding in the woods, burst into the cabin and started screaming like a wild animal. After the dogs led Jake and the Sheriff to more of Charlie's remains that were hidden in a hollow stump, the Sheriff arrested Frankie and charged her with murder.

At her trial Frankie pled not guilty, but the all-male jury convicted her, and Judge Donnell sentenced her to die. Due to North Carolina law she was not allowed to testify at her own trial. The sentence was appealed, but it was sustained by Judge Ruffin.

Frankie was not without her supporters. Thirty-four women from the community signed a petition to set her free, but Governor David L. Swain refused to grant a pardon. Even though seven members of the jury signed a petition saying they didn't think she should be hanged, the governor made no response.

With all appeals exhausted and the execution date fast approaching, Frankie's father bribed the jailer and spirited Frankie out of jail. As a disguise, Frankie cut her hair short and dressed up in men's clothes. She even wore an old felt hat. After leaving Morganton in an old hay wagon, they

FRANKIE SILVERS (CONT.)

were approached by the Sheriff who was suspicious. "Where are you going, Frankie?" Frankie replied in as low a voice as she could muster, "Well, thank you Sir, my name is Tom." Frankie's uncle, who was also in the wagon, said, "Yes, Sir, her name is Tom."

Mars Hill College

People came from miles around to witness the hanging. Her last request was a piece of cake, which was soon brought to her. Before she was hanged, they asked if she had anything to say. She said she did, but when she started to speak, her father hollered, "Die with it in you Frankie, die with it in you." So, she closed her mouth, and never said another word. Instead, she pulled the black mask down over her face. She was hanged July 12, 1833.

Some claimed that after the execution, Frankie's family became cursed. Her father was killed by the falling limb of a tree, and her mother died from the bite of a copperhead. Her brother moved to Kentucky where he was tried and convicted as a horse thief and hanged.

FRANKIE SILVERS (CONT.)

Some stories claim that Frankie herself composed the ballad known as "Frankie Silvers," and sang it from the scaffold. Alfred Silver, interviewed in 1903, claimed it was "printed on a strip of paper and sold to people who were assembled at Morganton to see Frankie executed." However, no examples of the broadside were ever found, and it was doubtful that a printing press existed in that region at that early date. The song was apparently first printed in a local newspaper in 1885, under the title, "Frankie Silver's Confession." However, one reader, Harry Spainhour, claimed that it was actually written by a 17-year-old co-worker named Thomas W. Scott. It is doubtful that Frankie composed the ballad. After all, she could neither read nor write.

When it was collected by Frank C. Brown of Duke University, the ballad was in 3/2 time, so I have put it in a more singable rhythm and have also changed the melody slightly.

Alice Lloyd College

"Don't swing a sledge to smash a fly." (1876)

FRANKIE SILVERS

This dread-ful dark___ and dis-mal day___ Has swept my glor___ ies___ all a-way. My sun goes down,___ my days are past, And I must leave___ this world at last.

Judge Daniel has my sentence passed,
These prison walls I leave at last.
Nothing to cheer my drooping head
Until I'm numbered with the dead.

Oh Lord! What will become of me?
I am condemned, you all now see.
To Heaven or Hell my soul must fly
All in a moment when I die.

I know his frightful ghost I'll see
Gnawing his flesh in misery.
And then and there attended be
For murder in the first degree.

His feeble hands fell gently down,
His chattering tongue soon lost its sound.
To see his soul and body part,
It strikes with terror to my heart.

You all see me and on me gaze,
Be careful how you spend your days,
And ne'er commit this awful crime,
But try to serve your God in time.

Farewell, good people you all now see
What my bad conduct's bro't on me.
To die of shame and deep disgrace
Before this world of human race.

"Pray for a good harvest, but keep hoeing."

GOODBYE TO MY STEPSTONE

In the 1890's this song was found in medicine show songsters such as *Hamlin's Wizard Oil* under the title "The Old Doorstep." I learned it in about 1971 from Jane Voss of California and have also heard it sung by Bascome Lamar Lunsford of South Turkey Creek, North Carolina, and also by Woody Guthrie. After singing it for thirty years, I've changed and adapted the melody.

I stand on my stepstone at evening time now,
Wind whistles by with a sigh,
Love now is gone as I stand here tonight,
And bid my old stepstone, goodbye. (Chorus)

It's hard to be parted from those that we love,
When reverses in fortune have come,
The world's strongest heartstrings are broken in twain,
By the absence of loved ones and home. (Chorus)

Pioneer Insult: *"He's slow as a schoolhouse clock."*

THE HOUND DOG SONG

Like the pugnacious lads in this song, people have been feuding about its origins for over 100 years. Also known as "You Got to Quit Kicking My Dog Around," it is claimed both by Arkansas and Missouri. Although it was published in 1912, the melody is similar to a much older fiddle tune, "Sally Ann."

Ev-ry time I come to town The boys keep kick-in' my dawg a-roun';
Makes no diff-rence if he is a houn', They got-ta quit kick-in' my dawg a-roun'.

Me an' Lem Briggs an' old Bill Brown
Took a load of corn to town;
My old Jim dawg, ornery old cuss,
He just naturally follered us. (Chorus)

As we drive past Johnson's store
A passel of yaps come out the door;
Jim he scooted behind a box
With all them fellers a-throwin' rocks. (Chorus)

They tied a can to old Jim's tail
An' run him a-past the county jail;
That just naturally made us sore,
Lem he cussed an' Bill he swore. (Chorus)

Me an' Lem Briggs an' old Bill Brown
Lost no time a-gittin' down;
We wiped them fellers on the ground
For kickin' my old Jim dawg around. (Chorus)

Jim seen his duty there an' then,
He lit into them gentlemen;
He shore mussed up the courthouse square
With rags an' meat an' hide an' hair. (Chorus)

LEATHER BRITCHES

If you said the words "leather britches" to a log cabin pioneer, he might take you to mean several different things. If he were a fiddler, he would say that "Leather Britches" was the name of an old fiddle tune that he had played countless times for square dances and frolics. He would tell you that this tune goes back to the Scottish reel known as "Lord McDonald's." With a grin he'd say that all the good fiddlers played it, and half the sorry ones, too.

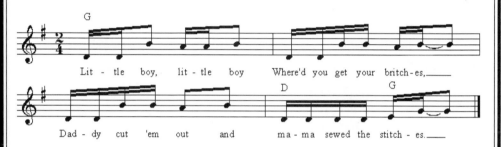

Lit - tle boy, lit - tle boy Where'd you get your britch - es,____

Dad - dy cut 'em out and ma - ma sewed the stitch - es.____

I went down town
I wore my leather britches.
I couldn't see the people
For looking at the peaches.

I went down town
And I got a pound of butter.
I came home drunk
And I throwed it in the gutter.

Leather britches, finger stitches,
Mammy sewed the stitches in.
Pappy kicked me out of bed,
I had my leather britches on.

Leather britches full of stitches
Old shoes and stockings on
My wife kicked me out of bed
Because I had my britches on.

If you were talking about "leather britches" with a pioneer woman standing in her kitchen or before the hearth, she would point to a string of beans drying near the fire. She'd tell you that she'd grown those leather britches in her big garden and that they were awful good eatin'. Before you knew it, she'd serve you up a bowl of them.

"The woman who invented grease gravy ought to have a monument a mile high."[49]

LITTLE LOG CABIN
IN THE LANE

When wind-up Victrolas became available in the 1890's, the only recordings one could purchase were classical, opera, comedy, or the popular tunes of the Victorian era. What you *couldn't* buy were the very sounds that people living in rural areas were most interested in hearing: Southern string bands and the old, sentimental ballads and songs. This changed suddenly in 1923, when a record distributor named Polk Brockman realized the untapped market for old-time music. He convinced Okeh Records to come to Atlanta to record the popular fiddler and moonshiner, Fiddlin' John Carson.

For his first song in front of the microphone Fiddlin' John sang "Little Log Cabin in the Lane." To the surprise of Okeh Record producer Ralph Peer, the song was an instant success. Demands started pouring in for more old-time music, so other companies dispatched recording crews to the South to capture rural stringband music.

The song that launched all this commercial activity, "Little Log Cabin in the Lane," was written in 1871 by William S. Hays. A professional tunesmith, Hays had the dubious distinction of spending time in a Union jail for writing "seditious" songs during the Civil War.

"There's no making a whistle of a pig's tail."

LITTLE LOG CABIN IN THE LANE

Oh I'm get-ting old and fee-ble and I can-not work no more, My rust-ed blad-ed hoe I've laid to rest, And my ma-ma and my pa-pa they are sleep-ing side by side, While their spir-its now are roam-ing with the blessed. Oh the chim-ney's fall-ing down, and the roof is cav-in' in, Let-ting in the sun-shine and the rain, And the on-ly friend I have left is this lit-tle old dog of mine, In that lit-tle old log cab-in in the lane.

Oh the happiest times to me was not many years ago,
My friends all used to gather 'round the door,
They would sing and dance at night
        while I played that old banjo,
But alas, I cannot play it any more. (Chorus)

Well, the paths they have growed up
        that led us 'round the hill;
The fences have all gone to decay,
The creeks they have dried up where we used to go to mill;
Things have changed their course another way. (Chorus)

Well, I ain't got long to stay here, what little time I've got,
I'll try to rest content while I remain,
Until death shall call his dog and me to find another home
Than the little old log cabin in the lane. (Chorus)

"A smooth speech is like honeyed poison." (1876)

THE LITTLE WHITEWASHED CHIMNEY

In about 1980, I was considering including "The Little Whitewashed Chimney" in a book I was working on, entitled "The Backpocket Bluegrass Songbook." The first recording I'd heard of the song was a 1956 Starday recording by Bill Clifton, one of the pioneers of early Blue-grass music. I managed to find Bill's address, and wrote him a letter, asking for details of where he learned the song and any background information he might have on it. I never received a response, so the song was passed over in favor of another song that I had more information about.

In early January 2000, I was surprised to receive a phone call from Bill Clifton. He apologized for his tardiness in responding to my letter of 1980. In response to the new millennium, he said he had been cleaning out a stack of old letters, and decided that any letter that was twenty-years old deserved a personal response!

Bill went on to tell me what he knew about "The Little Whitewashed Chimney." He remembered learning it from Paul Clayton, who had heard it on the radio in the mid 1950's as sung by Big Slim, the Lone Cowboy, on the WWVA Jamboree out of Wheeling, West Virginia. Curious about the song's origins, in 1999 Bill Clifton asked Ramona Jones and her husband, Grandpa Jones, what they knew about the song. Ramona told Clifton that John Laird, of the Renfro Valley Barn Dance, had once told her that it was popular in the 1870's, but that it originated just after the Civil War. It was later published in 1931, in Bradley Kincaid's songbook, *My Favorite Mountain Ballads and Old-Time Songs*. Kincade indicated that he had learned the song from Doc Hopkins, but the composer was apparently a man by the name of Tex Fletcher.

"If the smoke from the chimney doesn't rise straight up, it's going to rain."

THE LITTLE WHITEWASHED CHIMNEY

Where the Mis-sis-sip-pi's flow-ing by the sun-ny south-ern shore, And the steam-boats come a puff-in' 'round the bend, There's a lit-tle old log cab-in with a grape-vine o'er the door, And a lit-tle white washed chim-ney at the end. I'm

Chorus

go-in' back, yes, go-in' back to the place I love the best, And the folks who want me all their own a-gain, In that lit-tle old log cab-in with the grape-vine o'er the door, And a lit-tle white washed chim-ney at the end.

I went away up north
Where they told me I would find,
Money hanging around
Like apples on the trees,
But like my sweetheart told me
There was nothing of the kind,
And the weather was so cold
I thought I'd freeze. (Chorus)

I can see the smoke arising
From that little chimney top,
And it welcomes me
And greets me on the breeze,
And I'll start out a-running
And I know I'll never stop,
Until I've landed in that cabin
On my knees. (Chorus)

"I'm too poor to paint and too proud to whitewash."

MARY OF THE WILD MOOR

Although some people laugh and call them "tear jerkers," sad songs are often appreciated by those who have lived hard lives. Originating in England, "Mary of the Wild Moor" has been one of the most popular "heart" songs.

It 'twas on a cold win-ter's night When the wind blew a-cross the wild moor,_ When_ Mar-y came wan-der-ing home with her child, Till she came to her own fath-er's door.

North Carolina Archives & History   Photo by Margaret Morley

Pioneer Insult
"He's too sorry to throw a rock at a snake."[49]

MARY OF THE WILD MOOR

"Oh Father, dear Father," she cried,
"Come down and open the door,
For the child in my arms it will perish and die
From the winds that blow 'cross the wild moor."

But the old man was deaf to her cries,
Not a sound of her voice did he hear,
Though the watch-dogs did howl, and the village bell tolled,
And the winds blow across the wild moor.

"Oh, why did I leave this fair spot
Where once I was happy and free?
I'm now doomed to roam without friends or a home
And no one to take pity on me."

Oh, how the old man must have felt
When he came to the door the next morn,
And he found Mary dead, but the child still alive,
Closely clasped in his dead mother's arms.

Half frantic he tore his grey hair
And the tears down his cheeks they did pour,
When he saw how that night she had perished and died
By the winds that blow 'cross the wild moor.

The old man in grief pined away,
And the child to its mother went soon,
And no one, they say, has been there since that day,
And the cabin to ruin has gone.

But the villagers point out the spot,
Where the willow droops o'er the door,
Saying "There Mary died, once a gay village bride,
From the winds that blow 'cross the wild moor."

Pioneer Insult
*"She's as superstitious as an old granny woman who smokes a pipe
and doesn't know the war's over."*

DAVY CROCKETT & THE OLD FIDDLER

It was November of 1835 when Davy Crockett was on his way to San Antonio, Texas to defend a fort known as the Alamo. While approaching the Quachita River in Arkansas, Davy and his traveling companions thought they heard the sound of a fiddle. Being both a fiddler and a renowned buckdancer, Davy went over to investigate. He thought he even recognized the tune as one called "Hail Columbia, Happy Land." As he drew closer, he heard the tune change to "Over the River to Charlie." The words were familiar to Davy.

> Over the river to feed my sheep,
> And over the river to Charlie,
> Over the river to feed my sheep
> On buckwheat cakes and barley.

As he approached the shore of the Quachita River, Davy was surprised to see an old man with a white beard fiddling as hard as he could, while his two-wheeled carriage sat in the middle of the river. As soon as the old man saw Davy, he put down his fiddle and shouted that his frantic horse was too spooked to pull the carriage out of the river. Davy immediately urged his own horse into the river and managed to lead the frightened horse back to the shore. Once they were on dry land, the old man explained that he was a preacher and that he had hollered himself hoarse before using his fiddle to attract attention. Since they were headed in the same direction, Davy rode along with the old preacher. After they had successfully forded the river, the old preacher again took up his fiddle. As they merrily rode down the road, the preacher fiddled while Davy sang along.[57]

Pioneer Insult
"He didn't know enough to throw rocks at chickens."

DAVY CROCKETT TOLD A LIE!

Log cabin pioneers always loved a good tale, especially the tall ones. One of the greatest liars of all time was Davy Crockett. In his Almanac, he bragged he had "greased the earth's axis with bear's fat, sailed up Niagra Falls on the back of an alligator, used a piece of sunrise as fuel to cook his bear meat, picked his teeth with a pitchfork, combed his hair with a rake, fanned himself with a hurricane, drank the Mississippi dry, greased lightning with a bottle of rattlesnake tallow, and slid down the slippery end of a rainbow." And THAT was all done before breakfast![36]

FRANK MAYO as "DAVY CROCKETT."

For a midnight snack, Davy Crockett "always took a sandwich composed of half a bear's ham, two spare ribs, a loaf of bread, and a quart of whiskey."[12]

ME AND DAVY CROCKETT

T he life of Davy Crockett was the stuff legends and songs were made of. This version of "Me and Davy Crockett" started out on the minstrel stage as a song entitled "Pompey Smash." It was published in numerous minstrel songsters in the 1840's. I learned it from Doug Elliott, who collected it from Clyde Case, an eighty-year old basket maker from Duck, West Virginia. As a boy, Clyde learned it from his grandfather.[14]

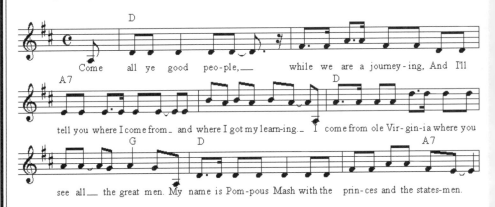

Come all ye good peo-ple,— while we are a journey-ing, And I'll tell you where I come from_ and where I got my learn-ing._ I come from ole Vir-gin-ia where you see all__ the great men. My name is Pom-pous Mash with the prin-ces and the states-men.

I'll tell you of a little hunt I had with Davy Crockett
He was half coon, half horse and half sky rocket.
I met him one day as I went out a-gunnin'
I asked him where he's goin', and he said he's goin' coonin'.

I asked him for a gun but he said he had none
Says I, "Uncle Davy, how'd you hunt without one?"
Says he, "Pompous Mash, just follow behind Davy,
And I'll soon show you how to grin a coon crazy."

I followed close behind till we came to a squirrel
Sitting on a pine knot eating sheep sorrel.
"Now stop! Stop still," and I began to feel,
Says he, "Pompous Mash, now brace against my heel."

I poked out my foot and I braced like a sinner,
And old Davy grinned very hard for his dinner.
He grinned away a while but squirrel didn't seem to mind it,
It kept eating sheep sorrel and never looked behind it.

ME AND DAVY CROCKETT

"Now," said Davy, "it must be dead,
'Cause I seen bark flying all around the thing's head!"
He climbed up the tree, this thing to disciver
All for the cause to mash Pompous Mash's liver.

When he got up to the place of the squirrel,
He was grinning at a pine knot big as any barrel.
Says he, "you black calf, you better not laugh,
'Cause I'll box both your ears and break you in half."

I set down my gun, laid aside my ammunition,
Says I, "Uncle Davy, I'll cool your ambition..."
Well then we locked horns and all my breath was gone
'Cause I never was squeezed so since the hour I was born.

We fought away half a day and then agreed to stop it.
For I was badly hurt and so was Davy Crockett.
When we stopped to look, both our heads were missing
He'd bit mine off, and I'd swallered his'n.

"Nostalgia ain't what it used to be."

MY OLD COTTAGE HOME

Although the Carter Family recorded "My Old Cottage Home" in the 1930's, I knew the song had to be much older than that. I finally found it in an old, weathered paperback gospel songbook, as written by A. A. Glen and J. H. Stanley. As was common in such songbooks, it was written out in "shape-notes." I still find it strange that the song appeared in a gospel songbook at all. There is nothing "religious" in the song itself, aside from the fact that it is about "home." My best guess is that "My Old Cottage Home" was written just before the turn of the century.

Many years have gone by since in prayer there I knelt
With dear ones around the old hearth,
But my mother's sweet prayer in my heart still are felt,
I'll treasure them while here on earth. (Chorus)

One by one they have gone from the old cottage home,
On earth I shall see them no more,
But with them I shall meet 'round the beautiful throne,
Where parting will come never more! (Chorus)

"The longest pole gets the persimmons."

COTTAGE PUDDING

1 cup sugar
2 eggs
2 cups sifted flour
1/3 cup shortening
    (butter or margarine)

3 teaspoons baking powder
$\frac{1}{4}$ teaspoon salt
1 cup milk
1 teaspoon vanilla

Cream shortening and sugar, add eggs, one at a time, and beat well. Mix dry ingredients and add alternately with milk to creamed mixture, beating batter smooth after each addition. Add vanilla. Spread batter in an 8" greased square cake pan and bake in 350° oven for 40 minutes. Cut in squares and serve with lemon sauce.[29]

Museum of New Mexico

Quilt Names

Log Cabin, Chips and Whetstones, Ice Cream Bowl, Swallows in the Window, Johnny Around the Corner, Toad in the Puddle, Circuit Rider, Rocky Road to Kansas, Drunkard's Path, Lazy Daisy, Turkey Tracks, Four Frogs Quilt, Fool's Puzzle, Wagon Tracks, Old Homestead, Cabin in the Cotton, Widow's Troubles, Grandmother's Dream, Trail of the Covered Wagon, Young Man's Fancy, Old Maid's Ramble.

RED ROCKING CHAIR

I n the mid 1930's, Bill and Charlie Monroe were making a name for themselves by crisscrossing North Carolina to perform on radio stations and at one-room school houses. After the Monroe Brothers split up in 1938, each went on to a successful solo career. Among the songs Charlie recorded was "Red Rocking Chair." Also known as "Red Apple Juice," it was actually an old Southern mountain song. The version presented here is what you might have heard in a log cabin in the 1880's.

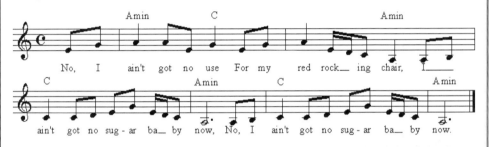

No, I ain't got no use For my red rock— ing chair, I ain't got no sug-ar ba— by now, No, I ain't got no sug-ar ba— by now.

Some old rounder come along
Took my sugar babe and gone,
And I ain't got no sugar baby now,
No, I ain't got no sugar baby now.

I gave her every cent I made
And I laid her in the shade,
And I ain't got no sugar baby now,
No, I ain't got no sugar baby now.

And it's who'll call you Honey
It's who'll sing this song?
Who'll rock the cradle when I'm gone?
And it's who'll rock the cradle when I'm gone?

Oh, I ain't got no use
For your red apple juice,
I'm living on your corn squeezings now,
Yes, I'm living on your corn squeezings now.

Photo by Wayne Erbsen

"He that handles thorns will prick his finger."

SHADY GROVE

A popular North Carolina banjo and fiddle piece, "Shady Grove" is also known as "Little Betty Ann" or "Salt River." Without a known composer, its verses float from song to song. An early version of the tune was collected as early as 1786 in a book entitled "Henry Beck's Flute Book."

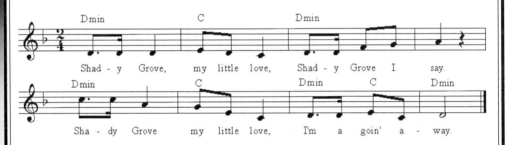

I went to see my Shady Grove
Standing in the door.
Shoes and stockings in her hands,
Little bare feet on the floor.

Wished I had a big fat horse
Corn to feed him on.
Shady Grove to stay at home
Feed him while I'm gone.

Peaches in the summertime,
Apples in the fall.
If I can't get the girl I love
I won't have none at all.

Lips as red as a blooming rose,
Eyes the deepest brown.
You are the darling of my heart,
Stay 'til the sun goes down.

Sixteen horses in my team,
The leader he is blind.
Ever I travel this road again,
There'll be trouble on my mind.

If I had a needle and thread
As fine as I could sew.
I'd sew that pretty girl to my side
And down the road I'd go.

Fifteen miles of mountain road,
Twenty miles of sand.
If ever I travel this road again
I'll be a married man.

Cut a banjo from a gourd,
String it up with twine.
The only song that I can play
Is "Wish that gal was mine."

*"I had so many blankets on the bed,
I had to get out of bed just to turn over."*

SOURWOOD MOUNTAIN

Albert Hash, the legendary fiddler from Whitetop Mountain, Virginia, once told me a story about "Sourwood Mountain." A couple was about to be married, so the young man went up on Sourwood Mountain and built a log cabin. On their wedding day, the fiddler played this tune, which has since been known as "Sourwood Mountain." Although there is no way to "prove" this story, it is the best account I've heard, so I'm sticking with it.

Chick-ens crow-in' on Sour-wood Moun-tain, Hey ho a did-dle um day.
So man-y pret-ty girls, I can't count them, Hey ho a did-dle um day.

My true love's a blue eyed daisy,
Hey ho a diddle um day.
If I don't get her, I'll go crazy,
Hey ho a diddle um day.

Big dogs bark and little ones bite you,
Hey ho a diddle um day.
Big girls court and little ones slight you,
Hey ho a diddle um day.

My true love lives up the river,
Hey ho a diddle um day.
A few more jumps and I'll be with her,
Hey ho a diddle um day.

Samantha Bumgarner

"His fiddle went 'squeak, squeak' like a pig being yoked." (1844)

SUGAR IN THE GOURD

Found in collections as early as the 1830's, "Sugar in the Gourd" was one of the most popular Southern tunes played for both rural square dances and fiddle contests. The melody may have inspired "Turkey in the Straw." The "floating verses" can be found in other songs, including "Cluck Old Hen," "There Was an Old Soldier," and "Preacher in the Woodpile." It was first recorded in 1924 by Fiddlin' John Carson.

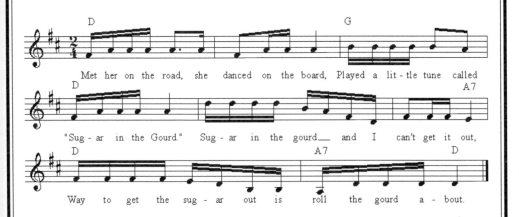

Met her on the road, she danced on the board, Played a lit-tle tune called "Sug-ar in the Gourd." Sug-ar in the gourd___ and I can't get it out, Way to get the sug-ar out is roll the gourd a-bout.

I had a little chicken she had a wooden leg,
Best dern chicken that ever laid an egg,
Laid more eggs than any hen around the farm,
Another little drink wouldn't do me any harm.

I went down in the old clay field,
Blacksnake grabbed me by the heel,
I turned around to do my best,
And drove my head in a hornet's nest.

Pioneer Wisdom
"Things are not like they used to be.
If things were now like they were back then,
The young people would starve to death."[8]
Lockie Richardson, 94

KING OF THE MOONSHINERS

North Carolina and Virginia have the dubious distinction of being the top producers of illegal hooch, better known as "moonshine." Far from civilized society, people in the backwoods have long had an independent spirit and often a careless disregard for the law. When store-bought whiskey was not available, some, known as "bootleggers," simply made it themselves. The most common component of moonshine, corn, was readily available, and so were apples and peaches, to make apple or peach brandy.

Mars Hill College

Although most moonshiners produced only enough to supply themselves plus their family and friends, a few reckless individuals were bent on large scale commercial production. The honorary title of "King of the Moonshiners" must go to Percy Flowers from Johnston County, North Carolina. In the 1950's and '60's, Percy had twenty men producing moonshine, often running their stills 24 hours a day. His income from moonshining was estimated to be $1 million a year. By openly flaunting the law, Flowers became almost a folk hero, like Robin Hood. Flowers added to his reputation by giving lavishly to the church and to those in need. Although he was frequently detained for breaking the law, he rarely served any jail time. Quite possibly, some law officers had a thirst that only Flowers could quench.

"I had enough liquor plumb in me to swim a skunk." (1858)

BEAR HUNTING WITH MOONSHINE

Dave Couch, of Sang Branch, Kentucky, told this bear hunting tale in 1951. "One old bear used to tear up Grandad's bee gums and rob 'em, so Grandad thought he'd just set a trap for that old bear. He got a trough and took him out about a half gallon of honey from a gum and got about a quart of moonshine whiskey. He mixed the two up and poured it all into that trough. He went out there the next morning and saw he had caught that old bear. There he was, laying drunk flat on his back, playing with his feet. Grandpa shot his brains out and got him another pile of bear meat and a good bear hide."[43]

Those Ornery Ozark Worms

"I dug a can of worms and headed for the lake. It was a hot summer day and my worms were drying out. I didn't have anything to wet them down with but a bottle of Ozark moonshine, so I doused them with good old moonshine. Arriving at the lake, I put one of those worms on the hook and tossed it into the lake. Right away, I had a hard strike and pulled in a nine pound bass. When I started to take him off the hook, I was shocked to find that he didn't bite the hook. Instead, the worm was holding the bass in

North Carolina Archives & History

the firm clutches of his teeth. I like to never have gotten the worm away from the bass. From then on, I always douse my worms with good old Ozark fighting moonshine."[42]

VOTING DRY

One time they held an election to decide if whiskey should be sold legally in the county. An official was tallying up the votes out loud, and he said, "Wet, wet, wet, wet, **DRY.** Humph! That must be that old moonshiner Huntley, who's afraid this new law'll hurt his business." He continued counting, "Wet, wet, wet, wet, **DRY.** Dad gum it! It looks like Huntley voted twice!"[41]

Great Smoky Mountains National Park

The Perfect Moonshine

Jess Young ran off an especially good batch of moonshine, so he gave his good buddy Bill Gouge a quart of it. Sometime later, Jess ran into his friend and asked him how he liked it. "That licker was just perfect." "What do you mean?" asked the moonshiner. "Well, if it were any better, you wouldn't have give it to me, and if it were any worse, I couldn't have drunk it."

"This liquor is so pure you can smell the feet of the lad that plowed the corn."[15]

DAD'S HOMEMADE WHISKEY

"**D**ad always kept an old stoneware jug of moonshine around the barn just in case he wanted a little nip, which was usually each morning and each evening. When we were young, he usually left it out where it could easily be seen, but when we got older, he wisely hid it behind a can of nails or under a rag, where he thought we wouldn't notice it. But, of course, we made it our business to notice things like that, and we frequently followed Dad's fine example and took a little nip or, more likely, a hefty swallow."

"One time, when we'd got a little heavy-handed with the jug, we were afraid Dad would find out, so we spiked the jug with some water, thinking he wouldn't notice. First mistake. Dad knew in an instant someone had been watering the jug, and he did what any good father would do in similar circumstances. He emptied the contents in a mason jar, and replaced the liquor in the jug with gasoline. He carefully returned the jug to its "secret" hiding place, smiling to himself that he had successfully baited and set the trap. 'Now let's see what it'll catch.'"

"Thinking we'd outsmarted Dad, we couldn't wait to get back to that jug. The next day, when me, Johnnie and Jack were in the vicinity of the barn, we went in there to get a little swallow of that good moonshine. I grabbed it first and without bothering to smell it, took a big drink. It didn't take me long to figure out what Dad had done, but I managed to swallow it without letting on something was amiss. Without cracking a smile, I solemnly handed the jug to John, who also took a big drink, and he too learned of Dad's prank, but he also managed to get it down without letting on. He handed it to our youngest brother Jack, who took a drink and immediately spit it out, yelling, 'Why didn't you tell me that this ain't liquor?' That cured us. We never again messed with Dad's jug."[38]

HOW TO HIDE YOUR STILL

Unless you're just plain stupid, you want to hide your still so the revenuers can't find it. The problem is they know where to look. The first place they look is up a holler near a spring of clear, cool water. That's because that's the best place for you to run your still. If you really want to be tricky, you can locate your still in a "dry hollow," far from the source of a spring, and run your water pipes underground from the spring. That way, you can locate your still about anywhere. If you run your pipes early in the spring, every kind of weed and vine will grow over it, and pretty soon, it will be nearly covered up. Of course, in the fall, when cold weather comes, falling leaves will also help cover up the water lines. So, if you don't get caught first, you can let nature do the work of covering up your water supply lines.

You can also make charcoal out of hard maple trees. Burning charcoal gives off an intense heat without the smoke. It's the smoke that's a sure giveaway as to where you're hiding your still. Hard maples were called "whiskey trees."

Of course, there are a lot of other ways to hide your moonshine still. One man I heard about bought a house right in the town of Hot Springs, North Carolina. It had a half basement, where he kept all his junk. After a year or two, he was running out of space, so he thought he'd enlarge the basement into a full basement. He took off some old boards, and you could have knocked him down with a feather. Behind the boards in the other half of the basement was a complete moonshine still! I never found out whether he took up production where the former owner left off.

*"This white lightning is so strong,
it would make a rabbit spit in a bulldog's face."*

MOONSHINE YARNS

A group of people were sitting around at the wake of a man who died the unusual death of drowning in a barrel of whiskey mash at the still he was operating. His wife was wringing her hands and carrying on in a pitiful way.

"I wouldn't take it too hard, ma'am," her husband's fellow moonshiner said. "I think he died happy. He got out and went to the bathroom three times before he died."[26]

Blue Ridge Heritage Archives, Ferrum College

An old deer hunter named Vick Divers had a keen thirst for whiskey, so he used to hang around and annoy the moonshiners until they'd give him a drink. One time he was up at a still, and the stopper came out of his powder horn. The powder started to dribble down the leg of his britches. When Vick wasn't looking, one of the moonshiners touched a hot coal to the powder and the explosion knocked Vick clear off his feet. "My goodness," said Vick, as he got up and brushed himself off. "That White Mule sure do kick!"[41]

"A sour faced wife is the liquor dealer's friend." (1872)

SHOELESS

Pioneer children went barefoot all summer and only wore shoes to go to church or school, if then. One time, a lad went to school proudly wearing his first pair of shoes. By the time he had walked several miles to the school house, his feet hurt so much he was limping. When he walked into school, the teacher took one look at his new shoes and said, "Johnny, you've got your shoes on the wrong foot!" "Sorry, ma'am, but these are the only feet I've got."[41]

In one part of Arkansas, it was claimed that nobody wore shoes. Some backwoods people there had never even

Great Smoky National Park

heard of shoes. One time, a passing traveler left a footprint in the mud. People started studying that footprint, but nobody could tell what kind of animal left its track. One enterprising boy built a pen around that footprint and charged five cents just to look at it![41]

Another time, two country boys took a load of pumpkins to town and were shocked to see most people wearing shoes. They didn't know what day of the week it was, but they finally decided it must be Sunday.[41]

"When you hear the first whippoorwill, it's time to go barefoot."

ONE-ROOM SCHOOLHOUSES

The teacher's voice was shrill as the students fidgeted in their seats. "Today, we're going to have a spelling bee, so boys get on this side, and you girls go over there." The young scholars laid down their slate boards and chalk and reluctantly took their places on opposite sides of the school room.

"I held my breath when the teacher called on me. 'ARITHMETIC.' I could feel my hands getting clammy and the blood draining out of my face, while my mind raced around trying to guess what the teacher was saying. I slowly began to remember a little jingle my older sister, Bonnie, had once recited to help her learn this very word: 'A rat in Tom's house might eat Tom's ice cream.' Saying it over to myself, I managed to recite 'A-r-i-t-h-m-e-t-i-c.' The teacher nodded her approval and went on to torture the next kid in line with another word."

Library of Congress

A traveler was trying to chat with a tightlipped farmer.
Traveler: "How far did you go in school?"
Farmer: "About 5 miles."
Stranger: "No! I mean what grade?"
Farmer: "Pretty steep."

ONE-ROOM SCHOOLHOUSES (CONT.)

Scenes like this happened a thousand times if they happened once in one-room school houses during pioneer days. These early schools were held in log buildings that often doubled as churches on Sundays. Schools had few, if any, windows to let in light, so the door was usually left wide open, even in the wintertime. A woodstove occupied the place of honor in the middle of the room. Recently, eighty-four year-old Eli Denny recalled that, when he went to school in the 1920's, "We had to saw the wood to keep the fire. We kids, we cut up the wood."[8] But, although conditions in these one-room school houses were rustic at best, most students did manage to learn their ABC's, their reading and their arithmetic, whether they could spell it or not.

One-room school houses were crowded with kids of all grade levels, so it did come in handy to have older kids helping the younger kids with their lessons. Sometimes the teacher would ask one of the older children to show the younger kids the way to the spring or to instruct them where to hang the dipper gourd after they got a drink of water. The older kids were even given the grim task of escorting their younger classmates to the outhouse.

Western Carolina University

"An empty sack won't stand upright." (1876)

ONE-ROOM SCHOOLHOUSES (CONT.)

For most pioneer kids, school was held no more than six months a year, if that. They were frequently absent during severe weather, when they had to help out at home with domestic chores, and at harvest time. In the 1930's, Aunt Cynthia Creasman, who was then eighty-five, was interviewed by Eilleen Galer near Asheville, North Carolina: "I went to school four or five years, but I was out a lot. Come wash day, I'd have to stay home and help Mammy with the washin'." She also recalled that, "you better not come in without your lessons. If you did, they'd set you in the dunce corner and anybody could laugh at you that wanted to."[20]

One little rhyme nicely illustrates how chores at home acted as a potent incentive to go to school:

Rather to school go
Than to corn hoe[49]

Despite the teachers' iron-fisted image as a person waving a paddle in one hand and a hickory switch in the other, most school teachers had a variety of tools to make students mind. Students who threw spit balls or paper wads might be required to write fifty times or more, "I won't throw paper wads." For infractions like fighting, being out of your seat, talking back to the teacher, or using foul language, the teacher might draw a circle on the black-

Photo by Wayne Erbsen

Bridge over Big Pine Creek

board, if there was one, and require the culprit to stand with his nose pressed against the circle.[22]

"I walked five miles to school, uphill both ways."

ONE-ROOM SCHOOLHOUSES

In these tightly-knit communities, teachers literally worked, worshiped, courted and married within shouting distance of their school house. Many teachers even boarded with families in the community. A whipping at school would be met with even more severe consequences at home that night. Thinking back to her own childhood days growing up in rural Virginia in the early part of the century, Mrs. Flora E. Edwards recently recalled, "Our teachers were strict and we were told to 'toe the mark.' That meant we all had to stand with toes up to a certain crack in the floor when we recited our lessons."[33]

Eighty-four year-old Eli Denny not so fondly recently recalled the hard puncheon seats he had to endure in his school during his youth. "They had no back rests at all and sometimes a mischievous boy would work a pin or a leg loose and out, and children and all would go over backwards."[8]

"All I had in my dinner bucket at school was some hickory nuts and a hammer."

CHILDREN'S GAMES (CONT.)

The kids usually had an hour break to eat their lunch, or, as most called it, dinner. If the weather was good, most would gobble their food in a hurry so they could run outside and play. The boys were likely to run foot races, play with balls, marbles, mumbly peg, pitch pennies, shoot off their pop guns, fire their sling shots or play leapfrog. Some boys threw what they called "shoulder stones." Many boys ran into the woods to hide behind trees, or pretended they were fighting Indians.

The girls, especially the younger ones, generally played separately from the boys. They were often busily involved in making playhouses out of sticks and rocks. The best doll beds were always made out of the soft green moss that grew at the base of the tall trees, which often shaded the play area. The girls were also very fond of playing jump rope.

Jump Rope Rhymes

Grandma Moses sick in bed,
Called the doctor and the doctor said,
"Grandma Moses, you ain't sick,
All you need is a licorice stick."

"Mother, mother, I am ill,
Send for the doctor from over the hill."
In comes the doctor, in comes the nurse,
In comes the lady with the alligator purse.

"Measles," says the doctor, "Measles" says the nurse,
"Measles" said the lady with the alligator purse.
Out goes the doctor, out goes the nurse,
Out goes the lady with the alligator purse.[15]

*"The road is wide and full of ditches, and someday I hope
I can patch your britches."* Autograph rhyme

CHILDREN'S GAMES

When boys and girls played together, they often played London bridge, hide and seek, blind man's bluff or drop the handkerchief. In 1997, 90-year-old Zetta Barker Hamby remembered her school years growing up near Grassy Creek, on the Virginia-North Carolina line. "When the weather was too inclement to go outside, we'd sit around the stove and sing: 'The Lone Cowboy,' 'Red Wing,' 'Rosewood Casket', 'Bury Me Not on the Lone Prairie,' 'Cripple Creek' and other songs. The boys didn't join in the singing much. It never seemed too cold for them to go outside."[22]

All Day Suckers

"We had an hour long lunch break at school, and Mr. Gordon Sturgill had bought the Wagg General Store and we had heard that he had "all day suckers." We were allowed to go down to the store if we were back in our rooms when the one o'clock bell rang. The suckers were one cent each, in flavors of strawberry, grape, orange and mint. My special friends and classmates, Hattie, Virgie, Eva and I would hurriedly eat our lunches and on good-weather days walk down to the store to buy our suckers...then we'd walk leisurely up the hill, hoping the suckers would last but be finished at the right time." Zetta Barker Hamby, 90.[22]

First student: *"Do you know why my teacher drilled holes in the paddle?"*
Second student: *"To make it go faster?"*
First student: *"No, to let the smoke out."*

Pioneer Insult
"He was so skinny he had to jump up and down to make a shadow."[49]

KNUCKLING DOWN TO
A GAME OF MARBLES

"When we had nothing better to do, we played marbles. The hardest part for us mountain kids was finding a place that was flat enough to play. On the 65 acre mountain cove that we lived on, the only flat part was right in our yard. We'd scrape away the grass and weeds and draw a square in the dirt with a sharp stick. In each corner we'd place a marble, plus put one in the middle, which was called a 'middler.'"

"Each kid had a shooter, which we called a 'taw.' The object of the game was to knock one of the marbles out of the square with the taw. We started the game by drawing a line in the dirt about two steps away from the square. Each of us would take turns shooting. If you managed to knock one of the marbles out of the square, you got another turn, and started shooting where you ended up. The one who knocked out the most marbles won."

"If you shot too hard, your taw would roll down the hill and you'd probably never find it. We had an expression that came out of this, 'He's lost his taw.' That meant that he lost something important to him."

"When you took aim to shoot, you were supposed to keep your knuckles on the ground. This is where the old expression 'knuckle down' came from."

"I've got what it takes to take what you got."

THE SKUNK IN CHURCH (CONT.)

A revival meeting had been going on for several days when some of the boys figured they'd do some hell raising of their own. It was decided that they'd "liven up" the meetings with either a hornet's nest or a skunk, whichever they found first. The boys headed out in all directions, each determined to find either a skunk or a hornet's nest. Finally, at the last minute, one of the boy's dogs cornered a wide-striped skunk in a rock pile. With some effort, the boy dug him out and got him into a sack. The sack and the boy were reported to be the stinkiest they had ever smelled. Since the skunk-catcher already stunk to high heaven, it was decided that he would get the high honor of dumping the skunk through the open window into the revival meeting.

Library of Congress

> *A skunk sat on a stump.*
> *The skunk thunk that the stump stunk,*
> *But the stump thunk that the skunk stunk.*
> Tongue Twister

THE SKUNK IN CHURCH

Western Carolina University

A full moon was shining as the boys approached the church. They could hear the preacher's loud voice booming out through the open window. Near the end of the service, the preacher said, "And bring us gifts." Then the church was quiet as the congregation began to pray. With the other boys egging him on, the stinky boy opened the sack and dumped the skunk through the open window near the front of the church. A woman in the first pew looked up and saw the skunk heading her way. She let out an awful scream right before she passed out. Then complete pandemonium broke loose as everyone ran for the closest door or window. The preacher jumped out the window, and nearly landed on the prank-playing boys. No one could ever recollect a church being emptied any quicker. All that was left in the church was the woman who had passed out, and the skunk.

Of course, the finger of suspicion fell on the stinkiest of the boys, but none of them would admit to anything, so as far as we know, their crime went unpunished.[38]

"A closed mouth catches no flies." (1876)

THE SHRINKING BRITCHES

This is a story of a young man who was proud as punch of his fancy new buckskin britches. He only wore them on special occasions, like when he was going sparkin'. The next time he went to see his girl, he put on his new leather britches, laced them up and headed out. Since he had no horse or wagon, he had to walk. It being wintertime, he was forced to wade two icy creeks and climb a mountain on his way to see his girl.

After he waded the first creek, his leather britches began to stretch and soon were way too big on him, so he took out his hunting knife and cut them down to size. Traveling on, he was forced to cross a second icy creek, and after emerging dripping wet on the creek's far bank, he noticed that again, his britches had stretched and were too big. Again, he laid the hunting knife to his britches until they fit snugly.

When he finally reached his sweetheart's cabin, his britches were the worst for wear, but he had come to court, and neither hell nor high water would stop him. Invited to come in out of the cold, the young man happily stood in front of the blazing fire and warmed himself. In a few minutes, steam started to rise out of his wet leather britches, and he was glad that they were finally starting to dry out. As his leather britches dried, they started to shrink and become hard. Pretty soon, the young man looked down in horror as his treasured, soft buckskin britches had become almost knee pants, and they were getting shorter by the minute! The young man excused himself and beat a hasty retreat from his beau's cabin before his pants could shrink up to nothing. He feared that, instead of wearing buckskin, he'd be buck naked! The young man and his girl were eventually married, but this story followed him to his dying day and was passed down through his children.[38]

"Trouts are not caught with dry britches." (1876)

THE JOYS & SORROWS OF CHEWING TOBACCO

"Chewing tobacco is old man's candy."[49]

Virtually all pioneer men, and many of the women, used tobacco. They either smoked, dipped snuff, or chewed tobacco, and many frequently did all three. One lad of six years decided he was old enough to seek the mysterious pleasures of chewing tobacco. His chance came when his father came home with a new wagon. On its maiden voyage the boy got to sit by himself at the rear of the wagon with his feet dangling over the end. Here he could magnify the joys of riding in a new wagon with the untested pleasures of chewing tobacco.

As the wagon started out, he bit off a big hunk and started chewing. But the wagon hit a rock in the road, and the boy almost tumbled out of the wagon. While trying to keep his balance, the boy swallowed the cud of tobacco. Immediately, his stomach felt like a volcano ready to erupt, so he slid down unnoticed out of the wagon and into the bushes, where he got sicker than a dog. He vowed that if he lived through this he'd never to touch tobacco again, and, as far as we know, he kept his promise.[38]

University of North Carolina at Chapel Hill

"How do you tell if a banjo player is sitting in a level spot?"
"The tobacco juice runs out of both sides of his mouth."

THE PEDDLER'S SACK

For many isolated settlers, a "store" was a humble peddler's sack. The news that a peddler was traveling through the area, often by muleback, was met with much excitement and anticipation. Those lucky enough to be paid a rare visit by a peddler treated him like a visiting dignitary. After spreading out the contents of his pack before the fireplace, he was usually offered the seat of honor, a meal and a bed to spend the night. His opened pack might reveal such treasures as cheap perfumes, exotic-smelling spices, sewing needles, combs, mirrors and other rare luxuries. As backwoods roads improved and more folks moved in, the peddler often graduated to traveling by wagon, so he could carry more merchandise and wouldn't need to return so frequently for supplies. Many of these traveling entrepreneurs dreamed of one day trading in their peddler's sacks and wagons for a permanent storefront.

Library of Congress

Peddler's Wagon

"When butter gets expensive, you learn to eat your bread dry."

GOING TO TOWN

When a pioneer family needed something it couldn't grow, hoe, or do without, it was time to go to town. A "town" in the early settler days was little more than a general store, a post office, a grist mill and a church. The post office could often be found inside the general store, and the church sometimes housed a school on weekdays.

When the roads were passable, going to town usually meant harnessing up the mule, horse or oxen and hooking up the wagon. 86-year-old Effie Price recently recalled that when she and her family went to church on Sundays, they usually found their neighbors alongside the road, dressed up in their Sunday best, waiting to catch a ride in the wagon.

Great Smoky National Park

Making a trip to town was often an all-day affair. Traveling the backroads, there would be creeks to ford, mud holes to get mired in and even downed branches and small trees to move out of the way. Of course, going to town was a major social event. You always saw friends, neighbors and relatives at the store or grist mill. There was news to catch up on, weather to speculate about and, for the men, a few lies to tell. Some of the men were even known to brag about the quantity of liquor they had run off the night before.

"Don't travel further than you can come back in one day on a mule."[49]

BACKWOODS BARTERING (CONT.)

For most backwoods residents, cash was something they rarely saw and seldom used. The destruction of the Southern economy at the end of the Civil War meant that what currency existed was worthless. But even though cash was practically nonexistent for most isolated pioneers, the enterprising spirit was alive and well. Instead of cash, most people relied on bartering. Peddlers and country stores traded their goods for any number of products of the rural homestead. Eggs, milk, butter, and hams were all readily accepted as good, or better, than hard

cash. Before the chestnut blight, many rural residents gathered chestnuts as a cash crop. Alice Hays remembered that a peddler used to come through Fines Creek, North Carolina, with a wagon. "He'd buy all the chestnuts he could, haul them to Waynesville, and ship them to Asheville. The dried chestnuts were sold for 5 cents a pound."[56]

Before tobacco became a steady source of income to rural farmers in North Carolina and Virginia, many depended on gathering roots and herbs, which were exchanged for goods or cash at the general store. Lockie Richardson, at the age of 94, recalled gathering polk root with her children. "We'd dig it, and then we'd take a little old hatchet and we'd cut it into slices, you know, and we'd put it up and dry it and then take it to the store."

"He would rather tell a lie on credit than tell the truth for cash."

BACKWOODS BARTERING

Photo by Wayne Erbsen

Some, like Bessie Greer, 88, sold wild cherry bark, sassafras roots and galax leaves. Della Maxwell, 79, recalls, "We gathered beadwood leaves, cherry bark, and boneset, which was used for colds. We also gathered elderberry flowers, lobelia, and slippery elm, which made a bitter tasting tea that was good for chills and fever. We also gathered, dried and sold pennyroyal, milkwood, and dock root."[36]

The scarcity of money in the rural economy was accepted as a part of life and did not seem to hinder business. Humorous stories, often based on true events, were told about it. One farmer crossed the mountains from his remote cove to sell eggs to a camping party. In exchange for his eggs, he was offered a dollar bill, but he refused to take it, as he had never seen one before.

"Where there are two people, there are customers."

THE GENERAL STORE (CONT.)

The very mark of civilization for backwoods settlers was the general store. Here was a chance to see, and maybe even purchase, the latest goods from far away places like St. Louis and New York. A typical store was jammed to the gills with every conceivable item necessary for the good life. There were cases filled with bustles and corsets for the ladies and stocking holders, paper collars and shirt fronts for the men. Glass counters revealed herb tonics, toilet and shaving soap, shoe strings, fish hooks and even bottles of morphine. For the kids, there were jars of penny candy. The aisles were crowded with plows, wagon spokes, coils of rope, axes, and sledge hammers.

A big pot-belly stove occupied the middle of the store. Around the stove was arranged a motley assortment of rickety chairs, apple crates and nail kegs. This was the uncontested gathering place for the retired philosophers, the loafers, and those who just wanted to get warm and catch up on the latest gossip and news of the day.

"It's easy to cut big hunks from someone else's cheese."

THE GENERAL STORE

University of North Carolina at Chapel Hill

It was at the general store where large amounts of tobacco was chewed and dipped, where the greatest hunting and fishing tales were told, and where the biggest yarns were spun. Not an hour went by without a vigorous discussion of politics, religion, crops, and of course, the weather. When somebody brought out a banjo or a fiddle, the old store invariably shook on its foundation as someone took to the floor to do some buckdancing or clogging steps. The back of the store was jammed with heavy barrels of whiskey, molasses, salt, lard, coffee, rice, vinegar and kerosene. Over the noisy din and clatter of the store, you could sometimes hear the irritated voice of the storekeeper yelling for someone to "Close the cover on the barrel!"

A stranger stopped at a general store and asked the loafers sitting around the checker board, "Why are all the farmers around here raising hogs instead of growing corn and tobacco?" One of the loafers looked up from the game and said, "Because you don't have to hoe hogs."[41]

A TALE OF TWO CHICKENS

Long before there was electricity in the valley, old man Jess McCool ran a small country store. To earn extra money, he sold chickens that he'd already killed and dressed and were ready to fry. Once a week he'd go to town and bring back a block of ice in his wagon. He put the dressed chickens in a barrel of water with the ice. So the chickens wouldn't go bad, every day he'd have to sell all the chickens he'd killed and dressed. Otherwise, he'd have chicken again for supper.

Late one afternoon, Hessie Blackman came into the store. Old man McCool knew Hessie to be one of his most finicky customers, so he braced himself when she asked, "Did you save me one of your plump fryin' chickens, Mr. McCool?" "Oh yes ma'am," he answered. "I sure did." "Well," she replied, "I believe I'll take one."

Jess reached down in the barrel, which he kept behind the counter, and brought out his last fryer and started to wrap it in a piece of paper. Hessie looked at it, and wrinkled up her nose and said, "That's a mighty scrawny looking chicken, Mr. McCool. Don't you have a little bigger one?" For Jess, this was the end of a very long and tiring day, and he was ready to close up the shop. Knowing she always bought just one chicken for her and her husband, Jess said, "Why yes ma'am, I do have a bigger one in here." He dunked that same chicken back in the barrel and squeezed the bottom, so it would look bigger at the top. "Here you go, Mrs. Blackman. How's this one?" Hessie scowled at the chicken for a full minute. Then she looked up at Jess who was staring anxiously at her. "This one's not much better than the last. But since my sister is coming over for supper, I believe I'll take both of them."[53]

"He that lies down with dogs must rise up with fleas."

CHICKEN POT PIE WITH SWEET POTATO CRUST

3 cups diced cooked chicken
1 cup diced cooked carrots
1 onion
1 Tbs chopped parsley

1 cup evaporated milk
1 cup chicken broth
2 Tbs. flour
salt and pepper to taste

Arrange chicken, carrots, onions, and parsley in layers in casserole. Combine milk and chicken broth. Add slowly to flour, blending well. Cook until thickened, stirring constantly. Pour over chicken and vegetables in casserole. Cover with Sweet Potato Crust, below. Bake at 350° about 40 minutes. Yield: 6 to 8 servings.

Sweet Potato Crust

1 cup sifted flour
1 tsp. baking powder
$1/2$ tsp. salt

1 cup mashed sweet potatoes
$1/2$ cup melted butter
1 egg, well beaten

Sift flour once, measure, add baking powder and salt, and sift again. Work in mashed sweet potatoes, melted butter, and egg. Roll $1/4$ inch thick and use as cover for chicken pot pie, above.

Berea College

"Always respect old age except when stuck with a pair of tough chickens." (1876)

AROUND THE HEARTH

"**O**ur land was so steep that the sun dipped behind our mountain by 6:00 o'clock in the evening during the winter. That made for short days, and long, cold nights. After the supper chores were done, wintertime found us huddled in front of the fireplace, trying to keep warm. We always kept a rip-roaring fire in the fireplace that would often crackle and pop, sending sparks and hot coals flying

into the room. When it was really cold, we'd roast on one side and freeze on the other. Even during a snowstorm, we kept the front door wide open. I've seen many times when the snow blew right through the living room and into the kitchen. Papa just loved the outdoors, and hated to be penned in, so when the cold wind and snow blew in the house, we just hunkered down closer to the fire."

Mars Hill College

"Mama always kept busy while trying to keep warm in front of the fireplace. She was always knitting, sewing, or mending some piece of clothing. Papa sometimes played the fiddle or banjo or told hunting or fishing stories. When he'd get carried away, Mama would give him "the look," and he'd tone his stories down some."

"Never remove ashes from the fireplace on Friday."[24]

OUR FIRST COOKSTOVE

Even though cast-iron wood cookstoves were available by the 1840's, it wasn't until the turn of the 20th century that they were common among most backwoods pioneers. Even after getting a woodstove, the hearth was still occasionally used for cooking dishes that didn't fit in the small ovens.

Albert Wilson remembers when he and his new bride bought their first cookstove as if it was yesterday.

> *"A couple at Cabin Creek were separating and were auctioning off all their belongings. The stove had cost $15 and was almost new, and they were asking $5. We wanted that stove but didn't have the five dollars. A man in the crowd heard that we wanted it and said he would lend us the five. A total stranger! So we got the stove, and, as soon as we were able, we returned the five dollars by registered mail."[17]*

Photo by Wayne Erbsen

"A big woodpile is like having money in the bank."

BORROWING FIRE

Alice Sloan, who was born in 1904, remembered one of her early chores growing up near Caney Creek, Kentucky.

"While Mama was out working in the garden, it was always my job to start the fire in the wood cookstove. I had to find a mouse's nest to use as tinder to get the fire started. A mouse's nest would make the best fire starter because it had cotton in it, as well as bark off of trees that had been shredded by the mice. Mama taught me how to stand the stove lid up edge-wise by that mouse nest and strike it until a spark would hit the nest in a way so it would catch. If the fire went out, I would have to go a mile or so to get fire. This is what we called 'borrowing fire.' A lovely saying came out of that: 'Well, what'd you come here for, a chunk of fire?' After I'd get my chunk of fire, I'd dash right back home and preserve it, so I could start my fire for cooking."[45]

"We were so hungry, we laid our ears back to eat."

Cookstove at the Old Crawford Place

Photo by Wayne Erbsen

THE STOVEWOOD BOX

"In the wintertime, one of my favorite places to hide was in the kitchen, behind the wood cookstove. There was just enough room for me and a couple of cats. One of the cats often beat me to the punch and would already be stretched out there when I arrived, but we all cuddled together. Besides being the warmest part of the cabin, it also smelled the best. It seemed like Mama was always cooking, so there were always great smells rising off the wood cookstove. Sometimes I got to be a taster before the rest of the family sat down to eat."

"The only drawback to hanging out behind the stove in the kitchen was that Mama didn't have far to go to find her chief wood gopher, me. Although I had a lot of chores, keeping up with the stove wood pile was one of my main jobs. I am here to tell you that the stove went through wood in a hurry, so there was a constant need to have just the right sized wood available at all times. Mama got mad as a wet hen when she was in the middle of cooking and stepped out to the porch to grab a piece of stove wood and the box was empty. I would 'catch it' then."

"After I had split the firewood into good sized chunks with a regular axe, I always liked using the hatchet to get the wood down to woodstove size. I had used that hatchet so much, it almost seemed like it was mine, but I had to be careful to return it to just the right place in the toolshed. Papa got mad when his tools were not where he expected them to be, and I learned to respect that. When I wasn't in a big rush, which was almost never, I would rub a little oil on the hatchet with a dirty rag, the way Papa showed me. Tools had a way of rusting really fast, so I knew Papa would be pleased when he'd find the hatchet well-oiled."

Pioneer Insult
"He was so stingy he could live on a soup bone for a week."[49]

TURKEY IN THE MOLASSES

Effie Price recently recalled making molasses at the Old Crawford Place in Big Pine, North Carolina in the early 1930's. After harvesting their cane, they hooked their old mule, "Mark," to the cane mill to grind the cane into molasses. As they were boiling the molasses in a big iron pot over an open fire, a wild turkey came along and jumped up on a limb that hung over the boiling pot. Just as the turkey was settling in, the limb broke and that poor turkey fell in that hot, boiling molasses. "You never heard such a ruckus in all your life," Effie said. "That poor, scalded turkey lost all its feathers, and we had to throw out the whole batch of molasses." With winter coming on, it was a wonder the naked turkey didn't freeze to death.

Effie & Dewey Price on WWNC radio

Molasses Crisps

| 1 ¼ cups flour | ½ tsp. ginger | ¼ cup shortening |
| ¾ tsp. soda | ½ cup molasses | |

Sift the dry ingredients. In a sauce pan bring molasses and shortening to a boil. Cool slightly. Add flour mixture. Mix well. Chill thoroughly. Cut in desired shapes. Arrange on greased cookie sheet. At 375°, bake until done, about 8 to 10 minutes. Makes about 2 dozen.[35]

"Expect a worm in every apple."

MOLASSES CAKE

½ cup brown sugar	½ tsp. salt
½ cup butter	¼ tsp. soda
½ cup molasses	1 egg
½ cup milk	1 tsp. cinnamon
2 cups flour	½ tsp. ginger
3 tsp. baking powder	

Cream butter, and gradually cream in sugar. Add molasses and beaten egg, and mix. Sift and measure flour, add baking powder, salt, soda and spices and re-sift together. Add flour and milk alternately and mix well. Bake in a well-greased shallow pan in a moderate oven - about 40 - 45 minutes. Serve while yet warm.[23]

Pack Memorial Library   Photo by William Barnhill

Grinding cane into molasses

*"If you need a helping hand,
you'll find it at the end of your arm."*

CORN

To log cabin pioneers, life seemed to revolve around corn. Even before their fields were cleared, corn could be planted around tree stumps and rocks. It thrived on mountainous land unfit to grow anything else but briars and weeds. Not only was corn essential to the pioneer diet, shucks were used to stuff mattresses and make cornshuck dolls, and cobs were used as smoking pipes, or even in the outhouse. Backwoods roads were often impassible, but liquid corn (moonshine) could still be transported easily and was commonly used as barter.

Ash Cake

2 cups cornmeal
1 cup buttermilk
$^3/_4$ tsp. soda

1/3 cup shortening
1 tsp. salt
Enough water to make
    a thick dough

Build up a hot fire. Pull out ashes and make a nest-like place in the ashes. Brush off ashes down to the hearth. Put your dough in the nest. Let it set a while and the dough will form a crust. Then cover with ashes and hot embers. Bake 20 - 30 minutes.[35]

Skillet Cornbread

1 cup cornmeal
1 cup all-purpose flour
1 tbs. sugar
3 tsp. baking powder

1 tsp. salt
1 cup milk
$^1/_4$ cup melted shortening
1 egg

Mix dry ingredients together. Melt shortening in oven in a cast iron frying pan. Mix wet ingredients together, then add melted shortening. Combine all, stir briefly and pour into hot greased skillet. Cook 375-400° for 20-25 minutes until browned.[51]

CORN SHUCKING BEES

Pioneer families grew so much corn they needed help with the shucking, so neighbors were invited in for a corn shucking bee. The mountain-high pile of corn was often divided in half, and a contest was held to see which team could shuck the most corn. Occasionally, fights broke out when unhusked corn was thrown on the other side. For the most part, however, corn shuckings were long-awaited community events. People got a chance to visit with friends and neighbors and occasionally be entertained by banjos and fiddles.

To spice up a corn shucking, a whiskey jug was often buried in the huge pile, and the one who found it was rewarded with the first "snort." When a boy found a red ear of corn he was allowed to present it to the girl of his choice, and she was obliged to kiss him, if he could catch her! Some sneaky boys were known to bootleg red ears in their pockets.

North Carolina Archives & History

"Pa always said that while he was alive, we'd never have to eat cornbread for breakfast."[56]

CORN COFFEE

Berea College

Desperate for a cup of coffee, one pioneer family was said to have learned how to make "corn coffee" from the Indians. They baked an ear of corn until it was burned black and then boiled it in a coffee pot. Yum! Others tried making "coffee" from parched barley, rye, wheat, even dried carrots. In 1867, Mrs. Nicholas Sharp, from Gage County, Nebraska, brewed a mixture of corn meal and sorghum to get a coffee-tasting drink.[43]

Whenever possible, settlers bought real coffee beans at the general store. At first, beans were only available green, so they had to grind it and roast it themselves. If they didn't have their own grinder, they often put the beans in a sack and mashed them with a hammer. Some homesteaders stretched out what little coffee they had by mixing two parts dried peas to one part coffee. Some even claimed they preferred this mixture over straight coffee, but I don't believe it.

> *"Sing at the table,*
> *Sing in bed -*
> *Bugger-man will get you*
> *When you are dead!"*

"If coffee grounds cling high up to the side of a cup,
company is bringing good news."

COOKING WITH CORN

Corn Oysters

1 cup flour
$^1/_2$ melted butter
3 Tbs. milk

2 tsp. salt
$^1/_4$ tsp. pepper
1 pint grated corn

Pour the corn on the flour and beat well. Then add other ingredients and beat well for three minutes. Have 2 inches of fat in frying pan. When smoking hot, put in the batter by the spoonful, holding close to the fat. Fry about 5 minutes.

Corn Dodgers, 1847

1 quart corn meal   dash of salt   water

"Use enough water to make the batter just stiff enough to make the mixture into cakes with the hands. Bake in a Dutch oven, on tin sheets."[44]

North Carolina Archives & History

*"Corn is not ready to grind into meal
until it's as dry as an old maid's kiss."[49]*

WOMEN'S TASKS

Candle making, canning, caring for children, carrying water, chopping wood, clothes washing, collecting honey, cooking, churning, doctoring, food preparation, gardening, grinding corn into meal, hoeing corn, knitting (socks, mittens, scarves), milking, herb collecting, putting up preserves, rope making from cornshucks, sewing, shoe making, soap making, spinning, stuffing mattresses, sugar making, washing dishes, weaving, wood chopping.[13]

University of North Carolina at Chapel Hill

Girls' Chores (1867)

Sewing, knitting, mending clothes, washing dishes, ironing, washing clothes, sweeping, trimming lamps, baking bread, general cooking, making butter and cheese, setting the table.[21]

Pioneer Insult: *"He'd steal money off a dead man's eyes."*

MEN'S TASKS

Mars Hill College

Cultivating fields, harvesting crops, tending livestock, trapping wild game, hunting, fishing, mending harnesses, cutting firewood, repairing farm tools, picking the banjo or playing the fiddle.[12]

Boys' Chores (1867)

Winding a watch, sewing on a button, harnessing a horse, greasing a wagon, driving a team, milking cows, shearing sheep, plowing, sowing grain, driving a mowing machine, swinging a scythe, pitching hay, whitewashing a wall, building a fire.[21]

"I helped my daddy clear the land. He wanted me to help him saw logs with a crosscut saw. I helped clear, helped plant corn, cut corn, shuck corn, anything he wanted me to do, that's the way I did. I don't reckon it hurt me. It might have helped me live longer."[36]
Mrs. Lockie Richardson, 94

Mars Hill College

"Beauty draws more than oxen." (1876)

BONNIE'S SEARCH
FOR BEAUTY (CONT.)

"**O**ne thing about my older sister, Bonnie. She was bound and determined to be beautiful, even if she like to kilt herself trying."

"Bonnie spent a lot of time in front of the mirror. Maybe she thought it was like looking down into a pond, where she might see some kind of a fish, or maybe a treasure chest that fell off some pirate's ship. Or maybe she thought she'd wake up one morning, look in the mirror, and she would suddenly become a raving beauty like the girls she saw in those magazines. Instead, all she saw when she got up in the morning was a sleepy-looking girl with her hair mussed up on one side from sleeping on it funny."

"Bonnie tried every cockamamie beauty recipe that came along. When she spotted a tiny wrinkle, she rubbed it with the juice of lily bulbs mixed with honey and white wax. Though she was born with straight hair and would always have straight hair, one day she got that determined look in her eyes and I knew it was the day for her to try to get curly hair. Reading from a magazine of beauty secrets she'd gotten in the mail, she got out a big bowl and mixed together olive oil, oil of oregano and oil of rosemary. All this she slathered on her hair and she sat there, waiting patiently for her hair to curl, but it never did."

"Pretty is as pretty does."

BONNIE'S SEARCH FOR BEAUTY

"When Bonnie got old enough to get acne, she asked her girl friends for a secret magic cure that would make it go away. She'd heard that eating molasses was good for acne, so every time we'd have biscuits, which was every day, she'd load up on molasses. All it did was make her fat. One day I about died laughing when I saw her rubbing slices of cucumber on her face. After she'd done that, she crushed up a perfectly good banana, and rubbed that on her face too. She looked practically good enough to eat, but the next day I could still see a few pimples poking out between the pieces of dried banana."

"When she'd go out in the sun, Bonnie's face would explode with freckles, like the rest of us. One old yarb doctor told her that to get rid of freckles she should wash in a maple stump on the first day of May. Yeah, I thought. But what about the rest of the year?"

"When she'd get down on herself, I'd try to cheer her up with this little poem."

> Ugly is to the bone;
> Beauty lasts only a day,
> Ugly holds its own.

Pioneer Insult
"She was so ugly her mother had to put a sack over her head before she'd let her nurse."

"Beauty won't make the pot boil."

HOW TO CATCH A MAN

• Steal a man's hat band and wear it as a garter. He will fall madly in love with you.

• Get your would-be lover to chew yarrow root or drink mistletoe tea.

• Go to the spring very early in the morning of May 1st. You will see the reflection of your future husband in the water. If no reflection appears, rush back to the house and look into your mirror at a sharp angle before speaking to anyone. You will see your future husband's face.[24]

• Count nine stars each night for nine nights, and you will dream of your future husband on the ninth night.

• Stare very hard at the brightest star in the sky and wink three times. You will dream of your future husband.

• When you hear the first coo in the morning at the spring, sit down and wait. You will marry the first man to pass by.

• Find a pea pod with nine peas inside and hang it over the door to catch the first single man to walk in.

• Count seven stars for seven nights and eat a thimbleful of salt before going to bed. You will dream of your future husband giving you water.[11]

• Kiss your elbow and you'll get the man you want.

"To cure love sickness: Eat a cucumber pickle."

YOU'LL BE AN OLD MAID

- If you ride a mule.

- Step over a broom.

- Sit on the table.

- Take the last biscuit from the plate.

- Cut your fingernails on Sunday.

- Spill salt.

- Cut off the right angle of a piece of pie first.

- Let anyone sweep under your feet.

To Dream of Your Future Husband

Look at the new moon over your right shoulder and say:

New moon, new moon, do tell me
Who my future husband will be.
What will the color of his hair be?
What fair day will he marry me?

She'll be Kissed If...

*Coffee grounds form a ring in the
    bottom of a cup.
A redbird or bluebird flies in her path.
She puts on a man's hat.
She makes a rhyme while talking.
She stumbles and kisses her thumb.
She kisses her hand after finding a
    spot of dirt on her face.
Her nose itches (by an old bachelor).*

HOW TO PICK A WIFE

• Women with small ears are stingy and whining.

• If her thumbs stick out, she will be a henpecker.

• If her hands feel cold, she is in love.

• If her second toe is longer than her big toe, she will be the boss of her husband.[40]

Avoiding Ugliness

"Drink coffee and you will be ugly."

"You will be ugly if the moon shines on your uncovered face."

*"March winds
And hot sun,
Make girls ugly-
And fellers run."*

To Get Rid of Freckles
• *Wash your face with rain collected on June 1st.*
• *Rub your face with a poultice of fresh cow dung.*
• *Apply water from a blacksmith tub to your face.*[40]

Pioneer Insult: *"She was so ugly she could stop a clock."*

DON'T TRUST A MAN IF...

- His ears grow too close to the top of his head.

- His beard is a different color from his hair.

- He jingles money in his pocket while trading.

- He doesn't make friends with a dog.

- He looks hard into his cup before drinking.

- He starts talking and forgets what he is about to say.

- He has "squinty" eyes.[34]

Uglying Squirrels

"While out hunting, I saw a strange-looking man wearing a large hat pulled down over his face. He was carrying three big fox squirrels, but he didn't have a gun. As he passed, I couldn't resist asking him how he managed to kill the squirrels without a weapon. He pushed his hat up so I could see his face. Whew!! He was the ugliest man I had ever seen in my life! He explained that when he sees a squirrel, 'I just raise up my hat, and I ugly them to death. I used to bring my wife along, but she just tore them squirrels up so bad we couldn't use them.'"[42]

Great Smoky Mountains National Park

COURTING, FRONTIER STYLE

By the time a backwoods girl turned 15, or a boy was 17, it was high time to get married. When a boy came to court in the winter, the couple was expected to sit by the fireplace with the entire family looking on. While the father spun yarns and the mother smoked her pipe, the young man was expected to declare his intentions on his first or second visit. After the rest of the family had gone to bed, the young couple would sit in front of the fire, "sparking." If it was especially cold, they would often get in bed together, fully clothed. This practice, called "bundling," was common on the frontier from 1750-1800.[10]

University of North Carolina at Asheville

"Lamp wicks crackle before a rain."

THE SATURDAY NIGHT BATH

"**E**very Saturday night, whether we needed it or not, we took a bath. The old metal washtub spent all week leaning up against the back porch wall, but on Saturday nights we moved it into the kitchen. We always fixed up a little curtain to give the one taking the bath a measure of privacy. Our Home Comfort cookstove had a water jacket, so Mama fired up the stove and when the water was good and hot, she'd dip out the water with a gourd dipper and slowly filled the tub."

"I'll never forget the winter my younger brother, Jake, was taking his regular Saturday night bath. He was nearly all lathered up when there came a loud knock on the kitchen door. It was our closest neighbors, the Rogers, with several of their kids, who had come over for an unannounced visit. They all crowded around the cookstove, and we visited and carried on, completely forgetting about Jake, who was shivering nervously just beyond the curtain."

Washtub at the Old Crawford Place

"Growing impatient, and not wanting to miss anything, Jake stood up on the edge of the tub to sneak a peek over the top of the curtain. But he leaned a little too far forward, and the tub gave way under him! Over he went, knocking the tub full of soapy bathwater all over the kitchen floor! Jake went flying through the air, knocking down the curtain and landing right in the middle of the floor, naked as a jaybird! Jake took off like a scared jackrabbit, and I don't believe I ever saw him run so fast in all my life! After that, Jake never seemed to take much of an interest in taking a bath again."[33]

MEN'S PIONEER FASHIONS

Crawford Worley, who used to live in our cabin, wore a pair of overalls every day of his entire adult life. He never had to wonder what he was going to wear when he got up in the morning. When he died, there was some discussion between his daughter, Effie, and his son, Dewey, as to how their father should be dressed at his funeral. Dewey thought a black suit would be the most traditional, but Effie finally convinced him that the most fitting clothes for their father to be buried in would be a brand new pair of overalls, so that's what they did.

Nuthin' Much to Say

Country people do not usually lack for words, but there was one eleven-year-old boy who had never spoken a single word in his life. His folks thought he might be a little lop-sided in the head, but there was nothing they could do about it.

One day, the boy was outside when he looked up to see a bull charging his dad from behind, so he yelled out, "Watch out for the bull, Pa!" The farmer turned to see that the bull was almost upon him, but he managed to jump a fence to get away from the bull. After the dust had settled, the farmer went over to his boy and asked him why he had never spoken before. With a sheepish grin the boy replied, "Before this, Pa, I never had nuthin' important to say."[41]

"In silence there is many a good morsel." (1876)

THE $50 LOG CABIN

I f you wanted a cabin built in Newton County, Arkansas around the turn of the century, Milas Wishon was the man to see. Besides being Justice of the Peace, Milas was an experienced log cabin builder. For a mere $50.00, he would build you a one-room log cabin, using only an axe, saw, hammer and froe. If he didn't have too many marriages to perform, he usually had it ready to move into in one week.

Photo by Wayne Erbsen

What has 4 eyes, 3 Heads, and 2 Tails?

A country boy went to town with only fifty cents in his pocket. There he met a city boy who asked him if he wanted to bet a dollar on answering a riddle. The country boy agreed, but explained that since the city boy was so much smarter and better educated than he was, it was only fair that he only had to pay fifty cents if he lost, but the city boy would have to pay a dollar. The city boy agreed, and they both antied up. The country boy then asked, "What has 4 eyes, 3 heads, and 2 tails?" City boy thought for a minute and gave up, so he handed the other boy a dollar. "Well, what *is* the answer?" he asked. "I don't know either," so the country boy handed the astonished city boy fifty cents.[41]

"Don't expect rain every time a pig squeals."

THE SOCKLESS POLITICIAN

L ike many early settlers, Joe Howard and his family lived their whole lives without electricity. Joe eventually became the Justice of the Peace and even won a term in the Arkansas state legislature.

On his first trip into Little Rock to attend a session of the Arkansas State House, Joe stayed in a fancy hotel that was fully equipped with both indoor plumbing and electricity. When it came time to go to bed, he looked around but couldn't figure out how to turn out the electric light that was hanging down in the middle of his room. He tried blowing on it, without effect. Finally, in desperation, he covered the light bulb with his only pair of socks. In the middle of the night, Joe awoke with a start only to find his socks smoldering from the heat of the light bulb. He managed to avoid setting the entire hotel on fire, but his socks were all but burned up. As far as we know, that was the first documented case in which a politician went sockless on the floor of the Arkansas legislature.[38]

Berea College

Fishing with Tobacco

A man was showing an old friend from Florida the fine points of catching fish in the mountains. He wadded up some chewing tobacco and threw it out in the lake. Immediately, two big bass jumped out of the water and swallowed the tobacco. In about a minute, when the bass came to the surface of the water to spit, he hit them on the head with his oar.[52]

"Keep your mouth shut and your eyes wide open." (1876)

HOW TO SELL A MULE

Jake Reaves was not at all happy when his wife's mother moved in with his family in their small cabin. She was an ill-tempered old witch who made his life miserable. One day the old lady went out to the barn to milk and accidentally backed into the hindquarters of Jake's mule, who had a disposition meaner than the old lady herself. The mule promptly kicked the daylights out of the old woman. After lingering for several days, she finally passed away.

Blue Ridge Heritage Archives, Ferrum College

When the family arrived at the funeral parlor, Jake was surprised to see a big crowd of men standing around outside. Pulling his wagon to a stop, Jake got down and approached the first man he met. Jake commented dryly, "I didn't know Grandma had so many friends." "We ain't here for the funeral," said the man. "We just want to buy that mule."

The Mule Trader

A mule trader and a farmer were haggling over a mule. The farmer bragged it was the strongest mule he had ever owned and demanded a high price. The mule trader hooked him up to his wagon to see for himself how he pulled. The first thing the mule did was run smack into a tree. "Why that mule's blind!" said the trader. "No, he's not a bit blind," said the farmer. "He just don't give a hoot."

"He and the devil drank through the same straw."

THE HAUNTED CABIN

Not far from her home near Mincy, Missouri, a lady noticed a cabin on a ridge where she had never seen one before. To satisfy her curiosity she got a big pair of field glasses, so she could see the cabin in some detail. She even saw smoke coming out of the chimney. However, the next day, the cabin was gone. Thinking this was odd, she asked the neighbors, but no one could remember there ever being a cabin at that site.[40]

North Carolina Archives & History

The Wood-Chopping Ghost

A cabin in the Ozarks was said to be haunted by a wood-chopping ghost. Those who camped near the cabin reported being kept awake by the sounds of someone chopping wood. When they investigated, they could find nothing. Some claimed that when the sound of the wood-chopping stopped, they could hear a grindstone being turned, as if the wood-chopper was sharpening his axe. Others said they heard the sound of water being poured on the grindstone, as if to cool it, yet there was no running water in the area.[40]

"It won't take long to curry a short horse." (1876)

THE PEDDLER'S GHOST

A peddler was said to have been murdered in a cabin in the Ozark backwoods many years ago. On February 2nd, the anniversary of the killing, a big blood spot on the floor becomes wet, as if by fresh blood. Anyone in the cabin on that date would see weasels, skunks, minks, wolves and even deer dash in the open door, plunge into the fireplace and then vanish up the chimney.[40]

The Two Grave Robbers

Two loafers were hired to steal a corpse from a village graveyard. They loaded the body into a wagon and covered it with canvas and straw. On their way to deliver the body to a medical school in Kansas City, they stopped off for a drink or two in a roadside tavern. While they were inside, a drunken country boy stumbled out of the tavern and decided to take a nap in the back of the wagon. He crawled in the back and covered himself with the canvas and straw and fell asleep. Just then, the grave robbers emerged from the tavern with a whiskey bottle to make the journey more jovial. As they traveled down the road, one of them turned and merrily shouted to the corpse, "Get up, old stiff, and have a snort." Never one to refuse a drink, the drunken country boy sat up with a jerk and said, "Don't mind if I do." This scared the grave robbers half to death! They took off running down the road, and I've not seen them yet.[40]

Log Cabin Superstition
Never sweep after dark and never sweep out the front door, because you might sweep dirt in the face of a ghost standing outside your cabin.[34]

THE GUARDIAN ANGEL

Geraldine Wild, who lived most of her life in Big Pine, North Carolina, recently told me the story of an unusual guardian angel who visited her family when she was a young girl, some eighty years ago.

Her brother Alvish took sick with an earache and a cough, and even his mama's home remedies did not cure him. Finally, her father, Levy Baker, saddled ol' Frank to go get some medicine from the nearest doctor, who lived way across the mountain in Spring Creek. To get there, Levy had to traverse a treacherous mountain known as Hardy Roberts Mountain. To make sure he was back before nightfall, he left early in the morning. He arrived at Doc Woody's house about midday, but the doctor was busy treating a man who had been injured by a gun shot.

By the time Dr. Woody gave Levy some medicine for his sick child, it was late in the afternoon. The sun would soon be setting behind the tall mountains. When he reached the top of the mountain, it was completely dark. Without a light to guide him or a trail to follow, he feared he would become lost. Just then, a little white dog appeared out of nowhere. Barking for ol' Frank to follow him, the little dog led them safely down the mountain. Just when he reached home, Levy looked around but the dog suddenly disappeared. Even to this day, some eighty years later, Geraldine believes the little white dog was a guardian angel sent down to guide her father safely over the mountain.

"A pig bought on credit is always grunting."

THE STRANGE BLACK DOG

When mixed with alcohol, feuding, romance and jealousy, backwoods dances sometimes became violent. At one dance in about 1900, the fiddler, Jack Lakey, was killed in Taney County, Missouri. Lewis Blair and another boy were sent on horseback to break the news to Jake's widow. As they rode along, a big black dog they had never seen before ran the entire distance to the cabin beside them. When one of the boys tried to hit the dog with his quirt, the whip slashed right through it, as if it were not there. When they arrived at Jake's cabin, his widow was standing outside her cabin, expecting them.[40]

Which Foot?

Sal was washing clothes in a big kettle in the front yard. While she was stirring the pot with a big stick, a stranger rode up and asked for direc-

The First Season

Harper's Weekly, June 8, 1878

tions. It was so seldom that she saw a man that wasn't her father or one of her brothers, that at first she didn't notice that she was standing on a red hot coal with her bare foot. They got to chatting, and pretty soon the stranger smelled something burning and yelled, "Watch out, you're standing on a hot coal!" Sal, whose feet were as tough as shoe leather, looked up at him and fluttered her eyelashes and asked, "Which foot?"

"It is good luck for a newly married couple to see a toad in their path."

GRANDPA'S FIRST BANANA

"**B**ack when I was a little boy, we'd never seen a banana. One time, we took Grandpa on a train and there was someone selling fruit. We said, 'Let's try one of these funny shaped fruits.' We bought one but didn't know how to get the darn thing open. Finally, we saw a man in the front of the car open a banana, so we got the banana open, but nobody wanted to take the first bite. Since

Western Carolina University

Grandpa was the oldest, we convinced him to take the first bite. Just as Grandpa was about to bite into the banana, the train went into a tunnel, and I yelled, "Don't eat that banana, it'll make you stone blind!"[30]

The $100 Dog

A man was visiting his cousin in the mountains and said, "Cuz, that's an unusual dog you have there. What is he?" "He's half hound and half bull, and he cost me one hundred dollars." The man looked shocked at that high price and said, "Which part is bull?" The mountaineer shot right back, "The part about the hundred dollars."

"Strive to be the kind of person your dog thinks you are."

THE LAZY PREACHER

There was once a good-for-nothing, lazy preacher who had an old hound dog who was even lazier than the preacher himself. In his prime, that hound could hunt with the best of them. But now, in his "golden years," the hound preferred lying around in the shade of an oak tree, snapping at flies when he could lift his head up that high. The only thing that got the old hound excited any more was when the preacher would play fetch with him. The preacher liked to whittle, and occasionally he would fling his whittle stick out into the yard. The old hound jumped up like a puppy and, with tail a-waggin', went and fetched that stick and brought it right back to his master.

On the preacher's farm was an old milk cow. In the summer, that cow would go down to the pond to drink, but when the pond would freeze over in the winter, the lazy preacher had to haul her up a bucket of water from the well.

One day the preacher had an idea. If he could chop a hole in the ice, then the cow could get her water there, and he wouldn't have to haul water up from the well. Then he remembered that stick of dynamite he had laid away to clear a stump. He put on a nice long fuse, lit it with the end of his cigar, and tossed it way over on the ice. Thinking it was just another game of "fetch," the old hound tore out over the ice to get what he thought was a stick. He picked it up in his mouth and triumphantly turned to return to his master with his prize. The preacher didn't waste any time but turned and ran like the dickens! He cleared two barbed wire fences with the dog in hot pursuit. Just as the preacher passed a white oak tree, that dynamite went off. It took about half the bark off one side of that tree, but the preacher was unhurt. The dog? Well, let's just say he went to another place to play fetch. And it looked like the old cow would be drinking out of the well bucket for a while longer.[32]

RATTLESNAKES IN THE BED

Though their names are long forgotten, this story still brings chills down the spine of those who are afraid of snakes.

In the fall of the year, a young couple picked out a perfect place to build their cabin. After clearing off the site, there was one large rock buried deep in the ground that simply would not budge. They finally decided that there was no harm in building their cabin right over it. Pity they didn't take seriously the mysterious hole in the rock. Instead, they decided that with winter approaching they could use the hole as a place to dump the ashes from their fireplace. What they didn't know was that they had built their cabin over a large nest of rattlesnakes that lived in that hole.

Several months after their cabin was finished, the first snow fell, so that evening they cleaned out the fireplace and shoveled the warm ashes down into the hole. Late that night the young woman awoke to find something crawling on the bed. She rousted her husband, and he got up in the dark to light the lantern to investigate. Before he could even get the lantern lit, he was bitten by several rattlesnakes who were crawling on the floor. The husband soon died, and the terrified young woman hid under the quilts as more rattlesnakes slithered over the floor and the bed. Her screams were finally heard by neighbors, who came over to check on her. There were so many snakes crawling around the bed, that they had to cut a hole in the roof to lift her out. No one ever went back there, and with passing years the cabin rotted away. All that was left was the rock and the stories about the snakes that lived there.[46]

"One southern town that was so rural that even the Presbyterians handled snakes."

SNAKE IN THE ATTIC

I'll never forget the time we had our own snake scare at our log cabin in Big Pine, North Carolina. It was just getting dark, and my wife, Barbara, and I were sending the kids up to bed. Then we heard our 14-year old son Wes' voice coming from upstairs. "Snaaaaake." There was a pause, and we heard it again, a little louder, "Snaaaaaaake." We were kind of frozen for a moment, and then it came again, this time louder than the last, "Snaaaaaaaaaaaaaake."

As we started up the stairs to the second floor, Wes told us to look up. There, almost hanging in midair, was a snake sticking out of a knot in the chestnut paneling. In a split second, it retreated to the attic and was gone. Though it was probably a harmless blacksnake, it didn't take much persuading to convince all the kids to sleep downstairs that night. And mum's the word about the snake. We don't want word to get out about a visiting snake in our house, or we'd never have any company!

"Mosquitos got so much of our blood, they were practically kin."

DANIEL BOONE & THE SCALPING KNIFE

Daniel Boone and his men had just finished preparing their evening meal. As they sat down to eat, they were surprised by a band of roaming Indians. Though the Indians acted friendly, Boone was suspicious of their intentions. He invited the Indians to join them in their meal but secretly warned his men to keep their weapons handy. After the meal, Boone approached the chief and asked to see his scalping knife. When the chief handed it over, Boone pretended to swallow it, and patted his stomach, as if he had just enjoyed a good dessert. Through another trick, Boone then "coughed up" the knife and handed it back to the chief, who eyed it suspiciously. Afraid of Boone's magical powers, the chief tossed the knife into the bushes, and he and his men arose, mounted their horses, and rode off in a cloud of dust.[36]

Once asked if he was ever lost, Daniel Boone replied, "No, I can't say I was ever lost, but I was *bewildered* once for three days."

HOW DANIEL BOONE SAVED HIS SCALP

While splitting rails for a fence, Daniel Boone was captured by a band of hostile Indians. Vastly outnumbered, Boone used his wit and told their chief that he would go with them peacefully if they would help him split one particularly stubborn log. He persuaded the Indians to have a tug-of-war and to pull the logs apart by the strength in their numbers. As the Indians got set to pull the log apart, Boone grabbed his maul and knocked out the wedge that held the log open. The log then snapped shut like a mouse trap, trapping the Indians' hands inside the log. Boone was then able to escape.[36]

"I am richer than the man mentioned in the Scriptures who owned a castle on a thousand hills - I own the wild beasts of more than a thousand valleys!" Daniel Boone

Pioneer Insult
"He's so crooked that when his pigs crawl through his fences, they come out on the same side."

STILL HUNGRY

An old man out hunting killed a big possum. He built a fire and cooked the possum up with some sweet potatoes. While his meal was cooking, he lay down and fell asleep. Some hungry boys happened by and heard the old man snoring. When they noticed the feast cooking over the fire, they helped themselves. Pretty soon they'd picked the possum clean and even ate most of the sweet potatoes. Before they left, they smeared possum grease on the old man's chin.

When the old man woke up, he felt the grease on his chin and figured he must have eaten the possum and then fell asleep. Then he felt his stomach and said, "I don't feel a bit full. That was the most unsatisfying possum I ever et."[41]

Western Carolina University

Pioneer Insult
"She was born in the middle of the week,
a-looking both ways for Sunday."

STEEPER THAN STRAIGHT UP

- "Our land was so steep, you couldn't walk on it. All you could do was sort of lean against it."

- "We lived so far back in the mountains that they piped sunshine in and moonshine out."[56]

- A Kentucky farmer fell out of his own cornfield and broke his neck.

- "Our farm was so steep I could look down the chimney and tell what the old woman was fixing for supper."[15]

- To keep his cows from falling off his land, one hillside farmer tied a rope around the neck of a pair of cows. He then pastured one cow on one side of the mountain, and the other one on the other side.[54]

- Our land was so steep, you'd skin your nose walking on it.

- Our land was steeper than straight up.

Berea College

> "It was so dark in our holler that we had to break daylight with a crowbar."[49]
> "Instead of getting the Grand Ole Opry on Saturday night, we got it on the following Tuesday."

RAILROADS & THE END OF THE LOG CABIN ERA

It was the railroad that first broke down the walls of rural isolation. The railroad not only brought in new people with different lifestyles, it also transported commercially made goods on a large scale. For log cabin dwellers, this meant the end of subsistence farming was close at hand. Instead of living only on what they grew, now they could sell their farm products to a regional or even a national market. Receiving money in exchange for the products of their toil, they could then use money to buy manufactured goods, which were also brought in by the railroads.

This dramatic change revolutionized the way rural people did business and the way they lived. Once truly isolated, the log cabin pioneer was now linked by the railroad to markets in all corners of the country, and beyond.

Courtesy of Douglas Walker

"A train is just a group of big stages hung on to one machine."
Davy Crockett

THE WIT OF WHISKEY

• "I spent all the money I ever made on whiskey, except for the little I wasted on groceries."

• "He used to run off the best moonshine likker in the country. When you took a snort of his whiskey, you'd better be standing on level ground."

• "When you buy a pint of likker, you're buying a club to beat your brains out."

• "It takes a whole pint of likker to prime him. That's when he starts into really drinking."

• "I'll bet my thumb that corn patch would 'still up a hundred gallons to the acre."

• "He's a quiet sort of man, but give him a few drinks and he's as loud as a jackass in a tin barn."[49]

Great Smoky National Park

Radio in the Backwoods

When radio came in, life suddenly changed. For the first time, isolated, backwoods settlers could hear the latest music, the news of the day, and be entertained by radio drama productions.

For those without electricity, a battery-powered radio soon proved be essential. When a family bought the first one in a community, their home suddenly became a gathering place to listen to the radio. Beginning in 1925, when the Grand Ole Opry came on each Saturday night, the kids were hushed, the dogs were shooed outside, and all ears were on the radio, as stars like Uncle Dave Macon, Deford Bailey and the Fruit Jar Drinkers hit the stage.

SURE-FIRE REMEDIES

- BIRTH CONTROL: Sleep with your feet in a churn.

- CHICKEN POX: Point the patient north and then run a flock of chickens over his body.

- COLDS: Tie a dirty sock around your neck. Kiss a mule.

- TEXAS CURE FOR COLDS: Mix one quart of whiskey and a dozen lemons. Throw the lemons at a fence post and drink the whiskey.[39]

- TO HAVE GOOD TEETH: Avoid cussing.

- HEADACHE: Hide several hairs from the sufferer's head under a rock for 7 days. Blow tobacco smoke in his ears.[24]

- SNAKEBITE: Find a madstone in the stomach of a deer. Soak it in warm milk and apply to the snakebite. Give the patient frequent doses of corn liquor.[24]

- BALDNESS: Apply a mixture of tallow and strappings of an old harness worn by a white mule.[34]

- TO QUIT TOBACCO: Smoke tobacco mixed with horse hair.

- RHEUMATISM: Apply an equal mixture of prickley ash bark, red earthworms and the oil of hog's feet.[10]

- TO BE PRETTY: Eat raw chicken hearts.

Publisher's Warning:
These remedies are provided as folklore. We do not recommend that you follow them to cure your own ailments.

SURE-FIRE REMEDIES

• COUGHS & SORE THROATS: Wear a flannel cloth saturated with turpentine around the neck. Make a tea of mullen flower, boneset, catnip, cocklebur, goldenrod, marigold, chamomile, wild cherry bark, or sumac berries.[24]

• TO BE HANDSOME: Eat a lot of chicken gizzards.[49]

• TOOTHACHE: Smoke the leaves of the plant Life Everlasting. Put a drop of oil of cloves on a piece of cotton and put on tooth. Chew yarrow leaves, mistletoe, bull nettle root or prickly bark.

• WHOOPING COUGH: Eat a piece of bread baked by a woman whose maiden name was the same as that of her husband.

• GAS: Raise your right arm up and down three times.

• FEVER BLISTER: Apply a billygoat's whisker to the sore.

• EARACHE: Put a drop of buttermilk in the ear.

• ACHING FEET: Carry a double cedar knot in your pocket or tie a salt mackerel to the bottom of your foot.

• CHAPPED LIPS: Kiss the middle bar of a five rail fence.

Photo by Wayne Erbsen

"Don't plow with a racing mare."

STAY WITH US!

There's an old expression, common in the Southern mountains even to this day, that you say when someone is leaving, "Stay with us!"

Some time ago, Joe Meadows was visiting an old mountain man way back up in a holler. Old man Phillips was telling bear hunting and fishing tales in front of the hearth. It started to get dark, so Joe said he had to be going, and he went to the door to leave. Old man Phillips stood up and said, "Stay with us," so Joe sat down again, and the old man told more stories. After a while, Joe felt he really had to be going and got up to leave, but the old man again told him, "Stay with us," so Joe sat back down, and the old man continued on with his stories. This went on several more times until old man Phillips himself stood up and said, "Heavens to Betsy! Ain't you ever gonna leave?"

Mars Hill College Photo by William Barnhill

"He can stay longer in one hour than any person I know."[9]

THANKS!!!

Many thanks to my wife Barbara Swell for sharing her love of log cabins with me and for editing, food consultation and wisdom. Thanks also to Steve Millard for cover design and Bob Willoughby for music transcriptions. Many thanks also go to family and friends for all their help: Janet Swell, John & Lori Erbsen, Beverly Teeman, Bonnie Neustein, Leann Erbsen, David Currier, Doug Elliott, George & Ted Hobart, Bob Hart, Ann Hoog, Jennifer Cutting, Bob & Patsy Allen, Loyal Jones, Harry S. Rice, Bill Clifton, George Frizzell, Richard Dillingham, Peggy Harmon, Mary Brown and the staff at Warren Wilson College Library, Valerie Minor, Laura Boosinger, Kerry Blech, Joe Cline, Peggy Seeger, Five Corners Publications, Eilleen Gardner Galer, Elaine Craddock, Pam Budd, and Eustice Conway. Thanks also to my neighbors in Big Pine, North Carolina for sharing their stories: Effie Price, Ray Worley, Bruce Buckner, Jake Owen, Geraldine Wild and John Weideman.

Berea College

"Advice that ain't paid for ain't no good."

PIONEER SLANG

A gone coon: someone who was ruined or lost
A whoop and a holler: a considerable distance
Arkansas toothpick: Bowie knife
Ballet: ballad
Blockader: a whiskey-maker or moonshiner
Booger Tales: ghost stories
Bushbreaker: someone who traveled in the backwoods
Bust a byler (boiler): to have a disaster
Cat head: biscuit
Catawampus: crosswise
Clabber headed: dumb
Cooter around: walk around aimlessly
Corn stealers or tater grabbers: fingers
Corn-fed: husky, strong
Dark-hearted: sad
Democrat: a yoke to keep cows from breaking fences
Devil's footwashes: hard rain
Doney girl: female sweetheart
Explatterate: to crush or smash
Feeling poorly: sick
Fiddle footed: footloose
Fiddle sticks: sticks used to beat out rhythms on a fiddle
Fish or cut bait: stop wasting time
Fleshen-up: to gain weight
Flustrated: greatly agitated
Froe: tool used for splitting or riving shingles
Frog sticker: large knife
Glut: wooden wedge
Granny woman: midwife
Half sole: a snack
Hant: a ghost
Hay-maker: a two pronged fork with a buckhorn handle
Hillside fish: hogs
Hit the shucks: go to bed
Honey-fuggle: to flatter for some selfish purpose
House-raising bee: when neighbors help to raise logs

PIONEER SLANG

Jimberjawed: having one's tongue constantly moving
Lambasting: a severe beating
Lank: hungry
Light and hitch: come in and visit
Light a shuck: move fast
Lit a rag: left in a hurry
Knot headed: stubborn or dumb
Make the fur fly: to fight
Make the chips fly: to work hard
Need-cessities: necessities
Obsquatulate: to mosey or abscond
Peart: lively
Polk: sack
Pooch out: to extend
Raise the steam: to become ardent or jealous
Rake up: remember
Ring-tailed roarer: an outrageous person
Ripped the sheet: to divorce
Rooster a gun: to cock a gun
Sang: ginseng
Sapsucker: a half wit
Sarsafari: legal proceedings of any kind
Scotch the wheel: put a rock behind a wheel
Shakes: wooden shingles
Shirky: lazy
Slack twisted: to lack courage
Slough footed: awkward
Smackdab: exactly
Sock dologer: in fighting, a lick that counted
Soup strainer: mustache
Split the quilt: to separate or divorce
Spootered: sputtered
Swarp: hit
Thunder-jug: chamber pot
Weaning house: a cabin where your just-married kids live
Yarb doctor: herb doctor[37]

SOURCES

1. Bealer, Alex, *The Log Cabin*, 1978.
2. Bennett, David, *A Study in Fiddle Tunes from Western North Carolina*, 1940.
3. Botkin, B. A., *A Treasury of Southern Folklore*, 1959.
4. Brown, Dee, *Wondrous Times on the Frontier*, 1991.
5. Brown, Frank C., *North Carolina Folklore*, 1952.
6. Charles Wolfe, *The Devil's Box*, 1997.
7. Clark, Thomas D., *The Rampaging Frontier*, 1939.
8. Cooper, Leland R., *Pond Mountain Chronicle*, 1998.
9. Cooper, Horton, *Mountain Folklore*, 1972.
10. Dick, Everette, *The Dixie Frontier*, 1974.
11. Dorson, Richard M., *Buying the Wind*, 1964.
12. Dorson, Richard M., *Davy Crockett*, 1939.
13. Duncan, Fannie, *When Kentucky Was Young*, 1928.
14. Elliott, Doug, *Crawdads, Doodlebugs and Creasy Greens*, 1995.
15. Emrich, Duncan, *Folklore on American Land*, 1972.
16. Everette, Edward, *Frontier Ways*, 1959.
17. Faris, Paul, *Ozark Log Cabin Folks*, 1983.
18. Fulcher, Bobby, "Traditional Dance on the Cumberland Plateau" in *The Old-Time Herald*, May-June, 1992 .
19. Galer, Eileen Gardner, *Appalachian Folk*, 1997.
20. Hale, Judson, *The Best of the Old Farmer's Almanac*, 1992.
21. Hamby, Zetta Barker, *Memories of Grassy Creek*, 1998.
22. *Home Comfort Cookbook*, 1933.
23. Jones, Ora L., *Peculiarities of the Appalachian Mountaineers*, 1967.
24. Jones, Loyal, *Appalachian Values*, 1994.
25. Jones, Loyal, Billy Edd Wheeler, *Laughter in Appalachia*, 1987.
26. Lavender, Linda, *Dog Trots & Mud Cats*, 1979.
27. Lilly, John, *Mountains of Music*, 1999.
28. Malone, Ruth Moore and Bess Malone Lankford, *The Ozark Folk Center Cook Book*, 1975.
29. McNeil, W. K., *Ozark Country*, 1995.

SOURCES

30. McNeil, W. K., *Southern Mountain Folksongs*, 1993.
31. McRaven, Charles, *Building & Restoring the Hewn Log House*, 1978.
32. Mirandy, *Tales of the Early Days as told to Mirandy*, 1938.
33. Moore, Helen K., *Pioneer Superstitions*, no date.
34. *Mountain Makin's in the Smokies*, 1957.
35. Murray, Kenneth, *Footsteps of Mountain Spirits*, 1992.
36. Nell, Varin H., *Word-Book of a Backwoodsman*, 1957.
37. Page, Tate C., *Voices of Moccasin Creek*, 1972.
38. Phares, Ross, *Texas Tradition*, 1954.
39. Randolph, Vance, *Ozark Superstitions*, 1947.
40. Randolph, Vance, *Hot Springs and Hell*, 1965.
41. Ring, Bill, *Tall Tales Are Not All From Texas*, no date.
42. Roberts, Leonard, *Sang Branch Settlers*, 1974.
43. Sara, *The Carolina Housewife*, 1847.
44. Shackelford, Laurel, *Our Appalachia*, 1977.
45. Sheppard, Muriel Earley, *Cabins in the Laurel*, 1935.
46. Shurtleeff, Harold R., *The Log Cabin Myth*, 1939.
47. Smith, Betty, N., *Jane Hicks Gentry*, 1998.
48. Still, James, *The Wolfpen Notebooks*, 1991.
49. Swell, Barbara, *Children at the Hearth*, 1999.
50. Swell, Barbara, *Log Cabin Cooking*, 1996.
51. Thomas, Lowell, *Tall Stories*, Lowell Thomas, 1931.
52. Thomas, Roy Edwin, *Come Go With Me*, 1994.
53. Welsch, Roger, *Shingling the Fog*, 1972.
54. Weslager, C. A., *The Log Cabin in America*, 1969.
55. Williams, Michelle Ann, *Great Smoky Mountain Folklife*, 1995.
56. Wolfe, Charles, "Old Hickory's Fandango," in *The Devil's Box*, September, 1962.

NATIVE GROUND MUSIC

BOOKS OF SONGS, LORE & INSTRUCTION

Backpocket Bluegrass Songbook
Backpocket Old-Time Songbook
Cowboy Songs, Jokes, Lingo
　'n Lore
Crawdads, Doodlebugs &
　Creasy Greens
Front Porch Songs, Jokes & Stories
Old-Time Gospel Songbook
Outlaw Ballads, Legends, & Lore
Singing Rails
Railroad Fever
Rousing Songs of the Civil War
Log Cabin Cooking
Take Two & Butter 'Em
　While They're Hot!

5-String Banjo for the
　Complete Ignoramus!
Starting Bluegrass Banjo
　From Scratch
Bluegrass Banjo Simplified!!
Painless Guide to the Guitar
Painless Mandolin Melodies
Southern Mountain Banjo
Southern Mountain Fiddle
Southern Mountain Guitar
Southern Mountain Mandolin
Southern Mountain Dulcimer
Children at the Hearth
Secrets of the Great Old-Timey
　Cooks

RECORDINGS

An Old-Fashioned Wingding
Authentic Outlaw Ballads
Ballads & Songs of the Civil War
Cowboy Songs of the Wild Frontier
Front Porch Favorites
Love Songs of the Civil War
The Home Front
Native Ground

Old-Time Gospel Favorites
Railroadin' Classics
Railroad Fever
Singing Rails
Songs of the Santa Fe Trail
Southern Mountain Classics
Southern Soldier Boy
Waterdance

LOG CABIN SONGS
is a CD/cassette of many of the songs in this book.

Write or call for a FREE Catalog
Native Ground Music
109 Bell Road
Asheville, NC 28805 (800) 752-2656
banjo@nativeground.com
www.nativeground.com